Ridin' SHOTGUN

How God Convinced Me to Ride with Him
on the Most Amazing, Incredible, Adventurous,
Miserable Journey of My Life

MARLI BROWN

WESTBOW
P R E S S®
A DIVISION OF THOMAS NELSON
& ZONDERVAN

This book is a work of non-fiction. Unless otherwise noted, the author and the publisher make no explicit guarantees as to the accuracy of the information contained in this book and in some cases, names of people and places have been altered to protect their privacy.

Scripture quotations taken from the Holy Bible, New Living Translation, Copyright © 1996, 2004. Used by permission of Tyndale House Publishers, Inc., Wheaton, Illinois 60189. All rights reserved.

All Scripture quotations in this publication are from The Message. Copyright © by Eugene H. Peterson 1993, 1994, 1995, 1996, 2000, 2001, 2002. Used by permission of NavPress Publishing Group.

Author photo: Heather Iafrate

WestBow Press books may be ordered through booksellers or by contacting:

WestBow Press
A Division of Thomas Nelson & Zondervan
1663 Liberty Drive
Bloomington, IN 47403
www.westbowpress.com
1 (866) 928-1240

Because of the dynamic nature of the Internet, any web addresses or links contained in this book may have changed since publication and may no longer be valid. The views expressed in this work are solely those of the author and do not necessarily reflect the views of the publisher, and the publisher hereby disclaims any responsibility for them.

Any people depicted in stock imagery provided by Thinkstock are models, and such images are being used for illustrative purposes only. Certain stock imagery © Thinkstock.

ISBN: 978-1-5127-1548-4 (sc)
ISBN: 978-1-5127-1549-1 (hc)
ISBN: 978-1-5127-1547-7 (e)

Library of Congress Control Number: 2015916682

Print information available on the last page.

WestBow Press rev. date: 10/30/2015

For Kennedie Morgan and Kadison Christian—
because more than anything,
I want you to follow Jesus and enjoy the ride.

And for Randy—
because, well, you know why.

Lord,
thanks for the adventure!
If I learned one thing on this journey,
it's that You *are* the journey.

Anyone who intends to come with Me has to let Me lead.
You're not in the driver seat—I am.

—Jesus

Contents

Foreword

I love viewing life through someone else's perspective, especially if they've lived an adventure that fascinates me. For years, my hubby has wanted to live on the road in an RV—kind of a footloose, fancy-free lifestyle that would take us on daily expeditions throughout America as I wrote and spoke. But we both hesitated to give up traditional living for the great unknown. Now that we are seasoned with years, we both wonder: What if we had?

So, I'm loving Marli's conversational writing style as she invites us into their family-of-four RV, where they lived for eight years. Pause … let that number sink in—*eight* years. That's impressive. That means being up close and personal 24-7. Add to that homeschooling, and now I'm thinking that all of them deserve an "above and beyond" award. Can you imagine the stories those children will be able to tell their children? They've lived the best kind of show-and-tell ever—indelibly seen, felt, and lived.

Did I mention that I have known Marli since little girlhood? (Not my girlhood but hers.) Her parents have been our dear friends for a hundred years, at least. I watched this gal grow up, marry wise, and begin a family. I've followed her family's travel blog and heard the woes and wonders of life they experienced on the road. Marli and her dear husband, Randy, have performed for us at our loved ones' homecomings and weddings. They matter to us, and after you read their story they will matter to you.

Marli and Randy are people of heart—singers and truth tellers, people worthy of being followed on the road, listened to on CD, and ministered to through the Word.

So step aboard, put on your seat belt, and be alert. There is so much to see and learn through Marli's side of the windshield. This woman has vision!

—Patsy Clairmont
Founding Speaker for *Women of Faith*,
Author of *Twirl* and *You Are More Than You Know*

Acknowledgments

Please accept my deepest thanks: Amy Loeffler, Dr. Gordon Ainsworth, Pastor Mike and Jandal Hefner for your influence; Dennis and Lorraine Pelley for your initial encouragement to tell my story; Jeff Jacobson for a great boost of confidence in a serious time of doubt; and Dr. Bob and Jane Turrill, president and CEO of the Evangelical Church Alliance; and the entire ECA family for the accountability.

Thank you to the Randy and Marli Ministries board of directors: Blythe Bieber, Pastor Rick Bosnack, and Cheryl Wilson. You have been an umbrella of support and direction, and we love you. Cheryl Wilson, there are not enough words to thank you for your service to the Lord. Dr. Hank Roso, former board of director's member, thank you for your investment of time and wise counsel. You and Holly mean a great deal to our family.

To the churches across the country who have opened your doors to our ministry, thank you for the honor of worshipping with you. Thank you to the pastors who have entrusted your flocks to our care for a few precious moments, and to our financial supporters—we would not be able to do what we do without your support. Thank you for investing in the kingdom and sending us.

Sarah Smith and the WestBow Press staff, thank you for your professionalism and partnership.

Patsy Clairmont, thank you for your kind words, encouragement, and friendship over the past forty years.

I must thank the many people who let me share their stories but whom I am unable to name—thank you for inviting me into your lives to watch as God convinced you to follow Him. (I recounted these stories according to my memory, so please forgive any errors in accuracy.)

To the Valade and Brown families—I love you all.

Thank you to my in-laws, Ron and Glenda Brown, for raising a man of God like none other. To the entire Brown family—it is an honor to share your last name.

Blythe Bieber, our family wasn't quite complete until you came along. Thank you for giving of yourself in so many ways. Your eagle eye is a gift and you have blessed me with editing everything from high school English papers to this book. Hopefully, it's gotten easier!

Jeff, Keli, Amber, Kierstin, and Celeste Hillier, thanks for everything. Each one of you makes my life exciting. You can thank *me* later for the stories I didn't tell. And girls—you always have a home with Auntie Mar Mar.

Mom and Dad, thank you for loving the Lord and serving Him even when people weren't peering in the windows. I didn't see everything, but I noticed a lot, and you did really well.

Kennedie Morgan, you were born as my daughter and are quickly becoming my friend. Thank you for picking up the slack as I wrote. Your celebrations when I finished a chapter made my day. I can't wait to see what God is planning for you—I know it is going to be amazing. You are pure sunshine.

Kadison Christian, thank you for watching out for your mama as we traveled the country. Your watchful eye has become a staple in our home; you are growing into a man of God. As a wise woman once said, "This one's a healer." You are special and unique, just like your name. In fact, there's nothing common about you. God has His hand on you, and I am certain you are great in His kingdom.

And last but far from least, I must thank the other part of me— Randy. You've seen me at my best and my worst. Your encouragement and motivation were not wasted. Can you believe I finished? Neither can I. Thanks for nurturing my gifts; there is no way to put into words how much your confidence in me means. I love you, babe. Now, can I have a day off? I'd like to do something fun.

God, You promised You would get me here; You kept Your end of the bargain, and I really appreciate the stories You let me live. Thank you for giving this simple girl indescribable joy. May all who read this have the same.

Introduction

"Shotgun!" We yelled it as we ran to the car in a mad dash to determine who would get to sit in the front seat. I usually won, not because I was faster or louder but because I had a terrible propensity for car sickness. That's why I got to sit in the passenger seat for much of my childhood, and eventually it became a habit.

I would sit in the front and look out the window. I was told to watch the horizon and not look down, to help alleviate my nausea. So I started out looking out the window to avoid throwing up, and forty years later, I am still sitting in the passenger seat enjoying the view.

In eight years of living in our 1994, thirty-six-foot Thor Ambassador motor home (with no other house), I only drove twice—once for about two hours and the other time no more than twenty minutes. Sure, I would pull the RV forward as Randy lined up the five-by-ten trailer door to unload our sound system into a church or banquet hall, but all I had to do was to put it in gear and pull forward slowly. I would look in the backup camera as I pulled forward until Randy made the stop signal. Then I'd step on the brake, put it in park, and turn off the engine. That I could do. Well, actually, I could do a lot more than that, but I didn't want to.

The time I drove for two hours, we were in the beautiful state of New Mexico, or maybe it was Arizona or Nevada; I can't remember. But I know there were mountains in the distance.

Randy had announced, "It's a Tuesday afternoon, low traffic, clear skies, and a straight highway. I've got to return a few calls to pastors, so you're gonna drive."

As I pulled onto the highway from the safety of the rest area, Randy sat on the edge of the passenger seat, giving me instructions and time to acclimate to driving such a big rig. With the attached trailer, we were forty-five feet long and thirty thousand pounds barreling down the expressway at sixty-five miles per hour. You can't stop on a dime, and changing lanes involves more than your blinker and rearview mirror. The ambient commotion of two kids wrestling and giggling, the wind howling, cell phones ringing, the dog barking, text messages dinging, and potholes and road rumble strips made for anything but a relaxed Tuesday afternoon drive. And I had to ignore it all while listening for anything strange that might be a warning to pull over.

Randy, talking with a pastor about an upcoming concert, gave me the thumbs-up sign, indicating that I was doing well. He pointed to the back of the RV and mouthed, "I'm going to lie down for a few minutes—but I'll be back."

I quickly pointed to the tiny mountain range far in the distance and whispered, "Don't be gone long!"

And then he left me.

Two hours later, that mountain range was no longer tiny; it was huge, and I was in it—in construction. There were no orange barrels, and I never saw a construction worker, but I drove through an endless narrow path of cement wall barriers. I thought to myself, *Well, the only thing I can hit is a cement wall.*

But I was still rattled, and I yelled to Randy while trying to concentrate on the center of the winding road. *Hands on ten and two ... ten and two,* kept going through my mind as I maneuvered between the cement barrier walls. Since there was no answer, I yelled a second, third, fourth, and fifth time. Nothing. I tried to raise the kids to no avail. *Where is everybody?* I wondered. I figured Kennedie and Kadison must have been in their bunks, watching movies with headphones that made it easier to hear the dialogue.

So there I was, driving the RV for the first time, in mountains and in construction with cement barriers not meant for forty-five-foot-long RVs. Whoever placed the walls there certainly hadn't considered me. Maybe they'd considered a seventy-five-year-old man used to driving his million-dollar Prevost bus across the country with nowhere to go but the next resort, but they surely hadn't thought of me. I was a first time RV driver, in a love-offering ministry with a couple hundred bucks in the bank. I have no idea what that point had to do with anything, but I remember thinking, *This is way above my pay grade.*

Both the cement barriers and the RV walls were closing in on me as the road twisted and turned. When Randy finally heard my cries for help, he came stumbling forward, rubbing sleep from his eyes. Had I been able to pull over, put the rig in park, and wait for him to finish his much-needed nap in the middle of that lovely Tuesday afternoon, I would have. But I couldn't. By then traffic had piled up, and we had to keep moving. Like cows in a herd. *Just keep driving, just keep driving.*

Randy took one look at me and started laughing. "Honey, I am so sorry! I fell asleep. Marli, loosen your grip on the wheel. It's okay, babe. You're doing great. Whoa—what state are we in?"

"I don't know," I said, with my eyeballs glued to the car in front of me, "but it's a state that has traffic, road construction, and *mountains!*"

As soon as it was safe, we did something I never want my children to do, but we did it anyway: we changed places while driving. With the cruise control activated, I slid slightly to the right while Randy jumped over the seat and grabbed the wheel. "Okay," he said "I got it."

Yeah, I definitely prefer the passenger seat.

The view is better there, and I don't have to worry about the surrounding chaos; I can enjoy the ride and let the driver do the work. But before you feel sorry for my husband, who drove me all over the country (or at least forty-five of its states, as of today), please know there was plenty for me to do. I had specific duties to keep me busy: I had to feed the family, homeschool the kids, pay the bills, answer e-mails, and keep the RV organized, not to mention do the laundry. And that was only the mundane, day-to-day mom stuff. I was constantly anticipating and preparing for ministry events. But all the while, I was watching.

I continually looked out the window and saw things: I saw the country, and I saw cities. I gazed at oceans and rivers and lakes. I saw people, and I saw inside their cars. I waved at babies riding in car seats, some screaming, some sleeping. I saw little kids motion for us to blow our horn (and watched them laugh at the wimpy, high-pitched *beep beep* it gave, because it never did work right). I saw people texting and driving; I saw people arguing, crying, and laughing. I called 911 when I saw a mother breast-feeding her baby, which was propped against the steering wheel, as she drove down the street. I saw rainbows and rode through snowstorms, sleet, and torrential rain. I never saw the wind, but I sure did feel it. I witnessed road rage and gawked at accidents. I saw dogs in cars, and horses, pigs, and cows riding in trailers, without a clue as to where they were going.

Riding around the country in the passenger seat, I saw more than I can recall, and I certainly can't remember everyone I met or even everywhere I went. But I do remember a lot of what I *learned*. Through those years, God convinced me to let Him take the wheel. He wanted to drive so I could enjoy the view as the landscape of His plans unfolded. As time went by, I gained a broader perspective of myself, even though it took a lot of convincing. I had to exercise my muscle of faith, and I still do.

The lessons I learned are far from complete, as I am still growing. At the outset, I didn't know how long the ride would last, and I certainly couldn't imagine what it would look like, but He convinced me to travel a road with Him different from any I had ever known. It was completely new and foreign to me. He gave us a simple ministry with a worldwide message of hope for anyone who would listen. I hope you enjoy the read as I share the most *amazing, incredible, adventurous, miserable* journey of my life.

BUCKLE UP

My Husband Said it Would Only Be for a Few Months

He did, but I didn't really believe him. He said if we moved into the RV full time, it would probably be for three to six months, until we settled somewhere. Randy and I knew it would most likely be a lot longer than a few months, but neither of us said that out loud. We just let the time unfold all on its' own.

Two years earlier, Randy and I had sold our house and moved into an apartment, which made it easier to travel with our national concert ministry. It was more convenient to turn the heat down, empty the fridge, load the RV, and go. We didn't have to think about mowing the lawn, shoveling the drive, or a million other things that come with owning a home.

Now, with two young kids in tow, it seemed the perfect time to break the lease on the apartment and move into the RV full time. Would it really be all that different? We were gone most of the time anyway. After a few years of serving in our concert and speaking ministry, we'd built enough relationships with pastors and congregations to book ourselves

1

almost every Sunday, along with weekday events. Marriage conferences had opened up, as well as women's events and banquets. Anything a church asked us to do, we tried. Most anything, anyway.

It was time to expand our borders and build relationships with pastors around the nation. We wanted to experience the country and discover what God was doing in other denominations. We desired to pull the body of Christ together, build bridges, and cultivate unity. Simply put, we wanted to encourage the church to stay faithful.

But to do that, we had to go, and to go, we needed to simplify our lives and move into the recreational vehicle. The word *recreation* means "fun"; it's something to do to *recreate* a feeling or experience. At least, that was my definition. And that was my husband's selling point.

"It's called a *recreation*-al vehicle. RV—get it? You like recreation; you like fun. I don't know anyone who likes to have fun more than you!" he told me.

And that's exactly how he did it. That is how he convinced me to sell a lot of our stuff, store the rest, and climb aboard the RV.

For eight years.

We're Off!

It was a blustery day in the beginning of January when we finished moving into the RV. After loading up clothes, jackets, and shoes for all seasons; cookware, office, and school supplies; instruments, toys, bedding, and books; and a million other things I didn't really need but thought I couldn't live without, I tried to wrap my mind around the situation. Leaning back in the passenger-side captain's chair, I took a deep breath and watched as my fearless leader put our rig into drive.

As we ramped onto the expressway to head south—or west, or maybe southwest (I probably didn't know—I rarely do)—Randy and I looked at each other and burst out laughing. It was the kind of belly laugh that makes you feel a little dizzy, like you need to breathe, but there's a nervousness that comes from somewhere, shows itself, and takes your breath away for just a second or two. I don't know why we laughed, but it was our response to a new way of life we knew nothing about. We had no clue how to live in an RV—what it would take from us or what it would give to us.

Any of it—all of it. We were clueless. Of course we were. We had never done it before. How could we have been anything *but* clueless?

"What in the world are we doing?" I asked.

"I have no idea!" he said.

We laughed some more and then just kept driving. And driving. And driving.

It was fun—really fun, and we felt free. I imagined tossing off the weight of the world into the deepest ocean and sailing across the surface with the wind blowing our hair wildly. It was romantic and scary and exciting and unknown. But we were together; we were all together. The three most important people in the world to me were within arm's reach. We had food, fuel, a bathroom, and our own beds. I was reeling from the adventure God had given us and excited to experience everything I could. It was a mysterious journey.

And besides, I didn't have to drive—Randy did. He loved it; he was beaming.

Watching my husband lead was thrilling. He didn't always know what he was doing, but at least he was confident. He'd been good at asking questions and reading manuals, but the questions and reading were done, and we were off. He led us confidently, cluelessly.

Now that the work of loading was over, the kids were thrilled too. They were ready to hit the open road with more stuffed animals than they could count. Honestly, after all the preparations, I was exhausted. I looked forward to crawling into bed after a hot shower and yummy dinner.

That was the first day. Then came the first night.

I Already Want to Go Home

We hit a snowstorm in Louisville, Kentucky. But let me backtrack for a minute.

Because I am from the Midwest, I *know* winter. Not just winter but blistering wind, ice, sleet, overcast skies threatening to blanket the ground with beautiful, glistening white water crystals that adorn tree branches like nothing else can—*that* kind of winter. During my fourth-grade year, we had a snowstorm that closed the town for at least two days; the snowdrifts were so high that we climbed up on the roof of our elementary school and made snow angels.

So like I said, I *know* winter—maybe not North Dakota–type temperatures, but I have had my fair share of winter cold. Actually, it's quite beautiful, and there's nothing like fresh snow to cover the dirty, slushy, trampled ground that needs a do-over. My favorite thing about winter is driving through a tunnel of trees just after a fresh snow. *Gorgeous* just begins to describe it. The other thing I love about winter's snow is a white Christmas. But other than that, you can have it.

As little as I love winter, Randy loves it less—much less. Growing up in the snowbelt of Cleveland, Ohio, he doesn't like the cold rattling his bones, and shoveling snow is a nuisance to him. Mowing his lawn is therapeutic, but shoveling his driveway is maddening. However, with a faithful furnace, good tires, a snowblower, and hot chocolate, anybody can make it through those five months. (It can kick off as early as November, and April often includes one last ice storm.) That's why we asked God to bless us with spending summers in the North and winters in the South— just like retired people.

Early on, we prayed about escaping the perils of traveling in a winter wonderland. We preferred to admire them from afar while watching the Weather Channel. Because of the necessity of travel in this touring ministry, winter would mean more than just cold winds and snow. For us, winter meant a new set of challenges: loading and unloading heavy equipment in the sleet and snow, and driving on icy roads in a fourteen-ton rig—all while pulling a car or trailer. It could be nerve-wracking.

Oftentimes we would drive several hours through dangerous winter conditions to make a concert, only to have very few people come, because of the hazardous roads. For many—especially senior citizens—even two miles of icy terrain can discourage the thought of going to church. And I understand. In that type of weather, I just want to hole up and wait for it to pass.

So we looked at our options, took a cue from the snowbirds, and asked the Lord to make a way for us to avoid traveling in the northern winter weather. The southern states had been very good to us, and we could fill several months with concerts. That's why we bought a motor home in the first place. But that first night, I quickly forgot the *why* of anything.

Back to our first night in Louisville, Kentucky.

Needing diesel fuel, our only choice was to pull into a truck stop where the snow was so deep that it pulled one of the front wheels of the car we were towing right off the dolly.

It was around midnight, and the trucks were big—a lot bigger than us. Randy lay on his back in the foot-deep slush—the kind of slush that sinks into your shoes and slowly creeps up the bottom of your jeans. A slush that's almost translucent from tires sloshing through it. The type of slush that seems to seep into your body and doesn't leave until you soak in a hot bathtub. Your feet get so cold that they go numb or feel hot and tingly.

I bent over, holding the flashlight so Randy could (somewhat) see what he was doing, but the wind was so blustery that my hands were shaking as I gripped the heavy, metal Maglite. The sleet slapped our faces, and I watched my husband shiver while his muscles tensed up as he tried to right the wheels. No one seemed to notice. And no one seemed to care. And then it hit me.

We were alone.

We put our kids in this rig we now called home, and we were alone.

Of course, we weren't, but it sure felt that way. And I didn't like it. I began to sniffle. The tears mixed with sleet added to the numbness of my frozen face. That's when I realized I wasn't as organized as I thought and should have left out a couple of those jackets for all seasons. Instantly, I wanted to go home.

"I ... I ... d-d-d-don't like it anym-m-m-more. I want to go h-h-home. C-c-c-can we go home?" The roaring of the nearby truck engines muffled my words.

Somehow, I forgot we no longer had a home to go home *to*. I was standing right outside my house (regardless of where it was parked), but I was beat and shivering and miserable, and I wanted something else. At that moment, I wanted *anything* else.

So the first night, I wanted to turn back. I wanted a shingled roof. I wanted the wind to stop, I wanted the sleet to end, and I didn't want to be cold, wet, and scared. It was the first night—the first obstacle, and I crumbled. I couldn't see past a tiny little snafu. The first one, only one so far, and I was done—I'd had enough. If I could have, I would have headed in the opposite direction.

Instead we went to bed. We turned off the engine and stayed right there in that truck stop. That was the first of many nights we would sleep in a truck stop, and eventually the sound of idling diesel engines would be a numbing sleep track for me. But not that night. That very first night, every sound those trucks made sounded foreign to me. And it seemed like they were mocking me.

You're in our territory now and we own this road. You're in a tiny RV reserved for retired couples twice your age who drive to Florida or Arizona and park in campgrounds to escape this kind of weather, and here you are in the middle of it, and you don't even know what you're doing. You are clueless. You are alone and helpless. You don't know how to live in an RV, and besides, you are terrible at geography. You never were any good at it, and now you travel full time ... ha-ha-ha. You will never make it. You will fail at this—and then where will you be? You won't even know because you are so bad at geography.

The Enemy

And that's when I recognized the voice. It was my enemy. With that last comment about geography, he took it too far. It was too personal. That heartless, intentionally cruel enemy, kicking me on the first night. He came out of the gates, swinging at my head and my heart. After all, our two most precious treasures were in the storm with us. We didn't check them into the nearest Hilton; they were right there with us. He wanted to scare me to death on that first night—to set a precedent he could use to derail me on this journey. And he would use anything—a storm, a car slipping off the dolly, a truck engine, a C in high school geography. Anything. He didn't care. Why would he? He's the enemy of everything resembling anything good, and he despises everyone made in God's image. He hates me.

I tucked the kids into their bunks long past their bedtimes (it was the first night of many with no reasonable bedtime), grabbed a pair of sweatpants and the thickest sweatshirt I could find, and fell into bed. I had no stamina whatsoever, no ambition to go anywhere but the familiar. And I had no problem admitting it. Forget all the prayer and planning; I was scared and weak, emotional and exhausted, overwhelmed and untrusting.

I told Randy I felt like crying—not sniffling, but crying.

"Babe, just go to sleep; it'll look better in the morning," he answered.

He was right. Sleep washed my mind, and the Lord's gift of peaceful slumber masked the sound of semis roaring past, not to mention the glare of their headlights. Eight hours later, I was a different girl.

The morning had come. *My* morning had come.

I often go back to that night. Freezing cold, alone, responsible for two kids, with little money, new to the RV—it was overwhelming and fantastic at the same time. I learned something really valuable that night: sleep is from God. He blessed me with deep rest. Sleep didn't change my situation, because in the morning, we still had to deal with the car, the dolly, and the snow. But it did change my perspective. A mind always works better with rest. After all, it was hardly a life-and-death situation. But that night, I had felt all alone. I wasn't, but I felt like it.

Have you ever felt like that? You know you're not alone, but you still feel lonely. You might be in a crowded room, but it doesn't matter; loneliness overtakes you.

Looking back, I think that night was a gift. Call me crazy, but those junctures push me to Jesus. Those are the times I lean on Him more than ever. Loneliness has a way of motivating us to fill the void with something. We all choose something or someone. Even with my husband, who is my best friend on the planet—the person I choose to be with over anyone else—I can be lonely. Why? Because even as wonderful as he is, Randy is not God. He cannot fill every need and void I have, because he is human and the need I have is for deity.

If you know me at all, you know I'm a simple girl who wants to know God. Really, there's not much more to me than that. I have no great ambition to be known or to accomplish a monumental task. But I *really* want to know God. I want to hear His voice and be led by His Spirit. I want Him to cure my loneliness.

I think it takes a while to discover why the hole is there and what to do with it. But I've found that God is the only One who can fill it and heal the loneliness. Without a house and far away from anything familiar, I found solace with Jesus. Nothing too complicated—just my Bible and a few minutes to cry out to Him.

I think we look for magic. People today want a microwave answer to an eternal issue. There is a space between God and man and there is no shortcut to knowing God. Jesus is the only way to know God the Father, regardless of what any newfangled philosophy might say.

Jonah

Jonah was a prophet who ran from God's plan. He ran long and hard, hoping to escape the watchful eye of his God, and as a result he experienced unbelievable isolation.

Let's review the story: The Assyrians were Israel's fiercest enemy, and the Israelites despised them. Within their oppressive empire, the Assyrians were evil, violent, and entirely against the God of Israel.

God told Jonah to preach repentance to the Assyrian people. But with a heart like Jonah's, that proved to be very difficult. He not only ignored God's request but headed in the exact opposite direction. While sailing from Joppa to Tarshish, his ship ran into a violent storm. Jonah 1:4 says, "But the Lord hurled a powerful wind over the sea causing a violent storm that threatened to break the ship apart."

That was quite a storm. The lives of everyone on board were in jeopardy, and the sailors cast lots to find out who was responsible. In those days, people were more likely than we are today to assume that personal actions were to blame for crises. The lot fell to Jonah, who quickly admitted he was running from God: "Throw me into the sea, and it will become calm again. I know this terrible storm is all my fault" (Jonah 1:12).

It's interesting that Jonah had compassion for these men. He couldn't have cared less about 120,000 Assyrians, but felt compassion for a handful of sailors he'd just met. He knew they were going to die if he didn't do something. At the same time, I think Jonah was so miserable running from God that he *wanted* to die. To Jonah, suicide was his best option—and it would save the other men.

The sailors didn't want to throw him overboard, so they tried to get to land. But as they rowed, the storm worsened. Finally, they threw him overboard, asking God to overlook their responsibility. The sea immediately fell calm. The sailors were in such awe of Jonah's God that they promised to serve Him. Jonah's sacrifice not only saved the sailors lives; it saved their souls.

But Jonah sank beneath the surface of wind and waves, not knowing the depth of the sea or what was lurking beneath him. Was he repenting? Was he saying his "if onlys"? Did he cry for his family? Or was he just relieved it was all about to end—the struggle, the running, the misery of disobedience?

And then—the great big fish. What was it like to be sliding down the throat of a fish? Picture yourself in its enormous mouth—nestled between rows of teeth—on a rough tongue, being sucked toward a gaping hole in the back of its throat. The smell, the panic, the fear of pain and death. Actually, death probably looked really good right about then. Struggling for oxygen and groping for something to hold on to inside a fish. *What now?* he must have thought. *How did I get here? Has my life really come to this? Am I really fish food? What else is in here with me?*

Three Days

A better question is not *what* but *who.*

To me, Jonah's life story is rich with redemption and miraculous intervention. God took hold of a man with a racist heart, a man who needed an infusion of God's compassion for the lost. Jonah took such ownership of his life that he said no to God's calling; that needed to change too.

God's plan for him included loneliness. It didn't have to, but it did. To reach Jonah, I think God let him feel some pretty awful emotions. For three days and nights, he survived in a fish. Think about that: a man was swallowed by a giant fish and then spewed out, alive, on dry land. Some think this is an allegory; I don't. I believe it actually happened.

Here's a funny thought: A lot of fisherman brag about the size of the fish that got away. With their hands wide apart, they proclaim, "I once caught a fish *this* big!" In the same way, I picture the fish that swallowed Jonah bragging to all his fish friends something like this:

"I once caught a man *this* big!"

"Oh yeah, what happened to him?" one inquisitive fish asks.

The giant fish admits, "Well, he upset my stomach, so I threw him up on a beach."

His fish friends swim away saying, "No way. I don't believe it."

On one of our many trips to the East Coast, we visited the American Museum of Natural History in New York City. We walked through an exhibit called *Whales: Giants of the Deep.* My mind immediately went to Jonah. Even though God doesn't reveal what kind of fish swallowed him, the exhibition gave me an instant understanding of the incredible size of some of the fish He created. The gallery hosted a full-scale model of a blue whale's heart; it was about the size of a Volkswagen Beetle. I watched my twenty-year-old niece Celeste walk through the chambers of the heart without even bending her head.

Learning that the heart of a blue whale could weigh up to fourteen hundred pounds made me wonder how big its stomach was. I then learned it takes twenty-two hundred pounds of food to fill the stomach of a blue whale. I quickly realized how possible it was for Jonah to have been swallowed whole. Was he floating in sea water and digestive juices? Was he treading water with half-eaten fish parts bobbing up against him? It was probably pitch black, with constant motion as the fish swam through the shifting tides of the sea. Most likely, Jonah was nauseated, and it had to stink. He probably wondered, *How did I get here? What are the chances?* Talk about a lonely roller-coaster ride of emotion! He thought he escaped God's call, but was targeted by God's storm. It seemed he was going to drown, but instead was swallowed by a fish. And while he was inside the fish, waiting to die, he had time to think—and pray.

> Then Jonah prayed to the Lord his God from inside the fish. He said, "I cried out to the Lord in my great trouble, and He answered me. I called to You from the land of the dead, and Lord, You heard me! You threw me into the ocean depths and I sank down to the heart of the sea. The mighty waters engulfed me; I was buried beneath your wild and stormy waves. Then I said, 'Oh Lord, you have driven me from your presence. Yet I will look once more toward your holy Temple.'
>
> "I sank beneath the waves, and the waters closed over me. Seaweed wrapped itself around my head. I sank down to the very roots of the mountains. I was imprisoned in the earth, whose gates lock shut forever. But You, O Lord, my God, snatched me from the jaws of death! As my life was slipping away, I remembered the Lord. And my earnest prayer went out to you in your holy Temple. Those who

worship false gods turn their backs on all God's mercies. But I will offer sacrifices to you with songs of praise, and I will fulfill all my vows. For my salvation comes from the Lord alone." (Jonah 2:1–9)

We have the benefit of reading the book of Jonah, but Jonah didn't. Whenever we read scripture, it's important to remember that the people involved didn't have the book as a narrative. Jonah was not following a manuscript; he was living it. He had no idea God was going to save his life, albeit through vomit. With digestive acids burning his skin, he probably thought he was going to die. And to the fish, Jonah was food intended for energy. But God didn't let that happen. The fish, not permitted to digest Jonah, got a stomachache and threw him up on the shore, at the time and place of God's choosing.

Did Jonah wonder, *Who is going to believe I was swallowed and survived for three days in the belly of a fish?* Or did he think, *On the upside, I have a second chance?*

His morning had come.

Jonah 3:1 says, "Then the Lord spoke to Jonah a second time: Get up and go to the great city of Nineveh, and deliver the message I have given you." In other words, God had to repeat Himself.

As I read that verse, I instantly think of numerous occasions when I failed to obey God the first time around.

Slow Obedience Is Disobedience

Jonah is a prime example of slow obedience. Nothing is more frustrating than telling my kids to do something three, four, and five times. (Actually, there is something more frustrating: overhearing another parent telling *their* kid to do something three, four, and five times.) In our household, we taught our kids that *slow obedience is disobedience*.

Jonah finally went to Nineveh with the warning of God's coming wrath, and the people repented. And then he complained because God relented. After all Jonah went through, he still wanted the people destroyed? Yep. He lacked compassion for his enemies *and* failed to see his own sin. You'd think God saving him out of the belly of a fish would springboard him toward grace. But not Jonah.

> Didn't I say before I left home that You would do this, Lord? That is why I ran away to Tarshish! I knew that You are a compassionate and merciful God, slow to get angry and filled with unfailing love. You are eager to turn back from destroying people. Just kill me now, Lord! I'd rather be dead than alive if what I predicted will not happen. (Jonah 4:2)

That's nothing more than a grown-up's temper tantrum.

The book ends with Jonah stewing in anger—pouting, in fact. God reveals His love for a lost city, all the while exposing the selfishness of a man. Jonah was more interested in God's wrath than in His help for lost people who needed a *morning*. And he was so obsessed with revenge that he ignored God's calling on his life as a missionary—a prophet, a chosen vessel of Jehovah God.

Isn't it funny that while Jonah was attempting to run from his calling as a missionary, he became one anyway? Not only did the sailors repent and turn to God, but the *entire city of Nineveh* did as well. The very thing Jonah didn't want to happen was accomplished through the compassion and love of God, in spite of His unwilling messenger.

Not only that, but Jonah's experience was a great foreshadowing of the burial of Christ. Just as Jonah willingly sacrificed himself to the mighty waves, so Christ sacrificed Himself to the cross. He willingly gave His life for ours, just as Jonah gave his life for the sailors. Furthermore, Christ went into the ground for three days; Jonah was beneath the surface of the sea for three days.

The story is about God's compassion for people. He brought Jonah up from the depths of the sea not only for the people of Nineveh but for Jonah himself as well. God's mercy for Jonah gave him another chance.

13

It took a long time for him to come around, but in the end, he told his story. I think he finally got it.

God rescued us too. While Jesus was in the grave, all hope seemed lost to His disciples. They must have wondered, *What now? We put all our hope in this one man, and now He's dead. Where do we go from here?*

And then the morning came. *Their* morning. *Our* morning. *All of creation's* morning.

Jesus breathed air again. He stood up and walked out of the tomb. His victory changed us forever. It changes our present situation, it changes our future; it should change our perspective as well.

The Backseat View

Years later, as I consider our first night in the RV, my perspective has changed. With certainty, I can say that God was more present than I realized. I think about His instructions and our dependence on Him. I think about our choice to follow Him. We needed Him to supply our every need, including compassion for others. We needed direction, instruction, guidance, money, rest, ambition, tenacity, and a whole host of other things I have simply forgotten about. In short, we needed Him.

I had to experience God as the driver of my life—without kicking and screaming. To encounter His grace and mercy in the middle of loneliness was a need I didn't even know I had, but He filled it anyway. It was good for me to obey without totally understanding. To say it was easy would be inaccurate, and to say we would do it all over again might be stretching the truth. But who knows? Maybe a day will come when He calls us to another kind of life and we'll have a decision to make. Maybe we'll have to sell stuff and store things and get rid of a lot of junk we no longer need. If that happens, I might have to reread my own book!

Let me introduce you to what I call "The Backseat View." At the end of every chapter, you will find a challenge. In this section, I want you to ask the Holy Spirit to personally apply what you have just read. Because this book is a testimony of what God has done in *my* life, it is important to give *you* an opportunity to look inward. Ask Him to reveal, confirm, encourage, convict, or meet whatever need you might have. When I read about Jonah, or any other person in the Bible who encountered God's power, I welcome those testimonies. I think God wants their stories to encourage us to investigate Him for ourselves. Another purpose of someone's testimony is to make us think about our testimony. So in this section, I ask you to "swivel your chair" and take a good look at yourself.

Sometimes, when we were driving down the highway, I would swivel my chair around to play a game with the kids or help with their homework. It was a different perspective, and I was able to accomplish something new. This is what I'm asking of you. Swivel your chair around and invite the Holy Spirit to evaluate and reveal your heart so you understand what God wants to do in and through you.

We all have a testimony, and I am honored to tell you mine. It would be wonderful if, when you finish reading this book, you are challenged to tell yours.

* Are you cold? Are you tired?
* Are you in the belly of despair?
* Does it seem like life's winter is stealing your stamina?
* Do you want to go home and hole up?
* Does a lack of compassion for others hold you back from your calling?
* Is loneliness so normal that it has become your sole confidant?

If so, it sounds like you need a *morning*.

> Sing to the Lord, all you godly ones! Praise His holy name. For His anger lasts only a moment, but His favor lasts a lifetime! Weeping may last through the night, but joy comes with the morning. (Psalm 30:5)

ENTRANCE RAMP

Small World

"Where are you from?"

To this stranger, it probably seemed like I didn't know, because I paused before I answered—and then was thankful when Randy, my husband of only eight months, jumped into the conversation to help describe the location of my small hometown. After all, how do you tell someone who lives on the opposite side of the world where Brighton, Michigan, is? Holding up my left hand in the "mitten position" and pointing to a western suburb of Detroit wasn't going to help me a whole lot here.

I don't recall where in Australia we were at the time, although I know it was somewhere near Melbourne. Randy toured as the keyboardist for the Christian rock band Servant, which took us to Australia during their summer—our winter. We saw kangaroos in the Outback, Melbourne city life, Wilsons Prom (the southernmost tip of Australia), and much more. We even made the jaunt over to New Zealand and stayed for a week. But that morning, visiting a Sunday worship service in a small country chapel, I never guessed I would leave the church humming "It's a Small World after All."

"We're from the United States," said Randy, "and we're here for about five weeks."

"Oh, where in America do you hail from?"

"Michigan, which is in the Midwest—although it's really closer to the East Coast than the middle of the country," I explained, silently wishing someone in authority would change the whole Midwest thing.

"We know where Michigan is. Where specifically are you from?" asked the Australians.

"Near Detroit," I said, and then added "Brighton," the name of the bedroom community where I was raised.

Quickly my mind diverted to the fact that when we moved there, I was in second grade and the tiny town had little more than a McDonald's and a post office. The Brighton Mall was so small you could walk from one end to the other in a matter of minutes, even while pausing long enough to see who was in the barber's chair and checking out the flavor of the week at Stroh's Ice Cream Shop. Today, Brighton is an upper-class city. Cities seem to take shape *after* I move away.

"We know people in Brighton!"

I couldn't believe it. Not only did they know the name of my quaint little village, but they knew a *live* human being residing there.

"Really?!" I exclaimed.

"A pastor by the name of Marv Valade."

All I could say was "He … he … he is my father."

It wasn't the first time I'd met someone who knew my parents from one ministry or another. These Aussies knew my father through Youth for Christ and had come to realize, as most people do, that my dad is not an easily forgotten man. His sense of humor (ironically his birthday is April Fools' Day) and compassion for others make him extraordinarily memorable.

There I was, ten thousand miles away from home, enjoying the freedom and independence of world travel, not to mention the feeling of being a newlywed, when all of a sudden I was reminded of where and from whom I had come. Ah, the life of a preacher's kid!

Fishbowl

I am one of the fortunate preacher's kids, affectionately known as PKs, who emerged from life in a fishbowl actually *wanting* to be in full-time ministry. That has to say something good about my parents. As you may know, a pastor's job is not easy and can be overwhelming. It seems there are always people with emergencies of some sort—domestic emergencies, financial emergencies, marital emergencies, hospital emergencies, mental emergencies—the list goes on and on.

Especially in a small congregation, needy people appear from nowhere and latch on to anyone who will listen. Many family vacations were interrupted with phone calls and people who needed something—even funerals. It was just tough to say no. Family dinners were disrupted when church people walked into the house without knocking. They figured since it was a parsonage and belonged to the church, they could let themselves in unannounced. We began locking the door, especially during the day. (In later years, my dad apologized for not setting stricter boundaries around our family life.)

The Appointment

When my sister Keli (pronounced *Keely*) and I were in our early years of high school, we anonymously made an appointment to see our father via the church secretary. At the scheduled time, we knocked on his office door.

"Come in!" he said in a cheery but tired voice.

Although thrilled to see his two children, he proceeded to tell us he had a scheduled appointment and we would have to make it quick.

"*We* are your appointment," Keli and I said, almost in unison.

The look on his face was one of confusion, guilt, and (ironically) relief. Our intent wasn't to inflict shame; we just wanted his attention, and we got it. My sister and I simply wanted him to know we felt like we were living on the back burner and it hurt.

One of the great characteristics about my dad is his listening ear. I can't say he was always focused, but I can say he heard us. In the following years, he spent more time at home and less time at meetings and appointments. There was more family privacy, and there were more phone conversations that ended with "Can we talk about this tomorrow at the office?" He separated ministry work and family life in a better way.

We were special to him, and he wanted to spend time with us. Not only did he value us as we were then, but he valued who we were going to become, and he wanted a hand in shaping us. That takes time and energy. To this day, my father talks about the "surprise meeting" we scheduled in his office, and how it changed his perspective; it was pivotal.

It's taken years for me to understand how to discern a true need as opposed to a situation that will just monopolize my time. And sometimes, I'm wrong. It's one of the things that makes ministry so tough—deciphering between a true need and an "I just really want some attention." But isn't that why we're in ministry? To help people in need? At the time, I didn't realize my parents had to learn that lesson. But while they were learning—I was watching.

I guess I didn't comprehend that they were young and maturing as normal people. As a kid, I witnessed how challenging ministry was for them, and I didn't understand they were on a journey themselves. I saw joy when someone surrendered to Christ, but I also saw disappointment when people made terrible decisions resulting in a mess. I felt stress when there wasn't enough money, and I witnessed miraculous provision from God. I watched my parents open our home to people in need and serve when they were depleted of energy. I marveled when God restored their strength and carried them through.

In our home, it was normal to trust God, normal to pray together, and normal to go to church; it's what we did. Although family devotions were haphazard, I could tell when they were going to happen, which was usually after breakfast when we had extra time *and* everyone was in a good mood. Dad would grab his Bible and *Daily Bread* booklet and flip to the date as I wondered whether or not the bacon would last through devotions.

My parents were hardly perfect, but as a kid, I had no expectation for perfection anyway. I didn't even think of perfection. They were just two people serving God who were learning themselves.

Faith Management

My heart breaks to hear a PK refer in disgust to growing up in ministry. How sad, and what a missed opportunity! My parents certainly made their mistakes, and not everything was balanced, but the older I grow, the more I see them as people who were serving the Lord while raising kids on a lot of faith and very little money. No matter what occupation your parents had when you were young, there was probably some fallout. Ministry is no different.

These days, it's easier for me to give them grace, because Randy and I are in the same situation. As we serve in full-time ministry while raising children, we experience many of the same obstacles: the challenges of time management, money crunches, spiritual trials, and the disappointment of investing in someone's life only to watch them walk away and reject the truth of Christ.

It's my turn now to experience much of what my parents went through and to learn to navigate the rough waters of full-time ministry. Since we don't want our kids to resent us for constantly investing in others (while they discover who they are in Christ), we've decided to *live* our ministry. It's not merely something we do; it's who we are. Ministry is much broader than a job or a position, although it's that as well. Ministry is a calling—for all believers, including our daughter and son. Therefore, instead of just going through the motions, we are learning to live our ministry, raise our kids, and mature as believers ourselves.

We pray the Lord will use Kennedie and Kadison not only to bring others to a saving knowledge of Jesus Christ but also to help them experience the spiritual growth that should happen after salvation—to make disciples, not merely converts. We pray our children will experience the intimate love of Christ and *know* their Creator. I don't want them to substitute "Christian service" for an authentic *relationship* with Jesus. Unfortunately, this common error is both subtle and damaging to even the greatest people of faith. It results in legalism and apathy, which at best eventually leads to nominal Christianity.

Since our goal is to raise godly kids who have an intimate walk with Christ, we must engage them in that—now. To give Kennedie and Kadison the best environment for learning Christ, we must know Him ourselves, and our walk must be genuine. Still, their surrender to the Lord is up to them. They must decide for themselves to be authentic, devoted Christ followers.

Over the years, and especially in the early RV days, well-meaning Christians (usually people who had never served in full-time ministry) offered advice on the perils of raising a family in ministry. We were warned on numerous occasions, "You can get too much Jesus," or "How long are you going to shelter your kids?" I believe many of those cautionary words stemmed from insecurity or maybe guilt over an unanswered call on their own lives. Whatever the case, we tried to answer carefully and not defensively (though I must admit, sometimes it was hard). In those instances, we decided it was more effective to let our lives speak louder than our words. I had to get comfortable with other people holding a differing opinion about God's plan for my life. Not everybody was going to understand or even agree.

Satan's devious tactics to thwart God's plan have destroyed too many families in ministry, resulting in wayward kids who eventually reject Christ. And yes, that could happen to us. Our daughter and son could make the worst of choices, walk away, and turn their backs on everything we've taught them—because, frankly, that is one of their options. Not only that, but because they are with us 24-7, *we* could ruin them! However, I pray daily that they choose the wise option of following Jesus and claiming their eternal inheritance.

The Cost of a Call

When God calls a person, a decision must be made, but not before the cost is calculated. Everything costs something; serving Christ is no different. In fact, a life of ministry is the most expensive kind of life to live. I don't mean in financial terms (although money helps) but rather in the quality of servanthood. Salvation is completely free, but true discipleship will cost you everything. Luke 14:25–33 says,

> A large crowd was following Jesus. He turned around and said to them, "If you want to be my disciple, you must hate everyone else by comparison — your father and mother, wife and children, brothers and sisters — yes, even your own life. Otherwise, you cannot be my disciple. And if you do not carry your own cross and follow me, you cannot be my disciple. But don't begin until you count the cost. For who would begin construction of a building without first calculating the cost to see if there is enough money to finish it? Otherwise, you might complete only the foundation before running out of money, and then everyone would laugh at you. They would say, 'There's the person who started that building and couldn't afford to finish it!'
>
> Or what king would go to war against another king without first sitting down with his counselors to discuss whether his army of 10,000 could defeat the 20,000 soldiers marching against him? And if he can't, he will send a delegation to discuss terms of peace while the enemy is still far away. So you cannot become my disciple without giving up everything you own."

We are wise to give serious consideration to the requirements of Him who calls us. Jesus wanted people to think about the cost of following Him.

23

Even He experienced a deep soul-searching in the garden of Gethsemane; it was inevitable. He considered His life, His death, and exactly what His Father asked of Him. There, in the middle of the night, Jesus counted the cost. He looked through time as only He could, and considered you and me. His mission was us, and He calculated the cost. We were expensive, but He valued our worth. I don't think we do.

One time when I was speaking at a youth camp in South Dakota, a little girl came to me before the service; she wanted to give her life to Christ. Anxiously anticipating the invitation at the end of the session, she said she planned to go forward. Instead of delaying this momentous event, I invited her to the altar right then.

"Do you want to go to the altar now and ask Jesus into your heart?" I asked the beautiful nine-year-old.

"Hmmm, okay," she answered, shrugging her cute little shoulders and quickly adding, "Oh, let me get my brother; he wants to do it too."

I giggled as she turned around and skipped off to find her younger sibling. Watching as they returned hand in hand, excited to make this life choice, I explained that the altar was not a magical place but rather a place of devotion (and death—but that seemed a little heavy for a nine-year-old).

"There is nothing magical about kneeling at the altar, and there are no magical words you have to say to Jesus," I told them. "It's all about your heart, and this is a wonderful place to lay your life down before God. Do you want to give Him everything right now and ask Him to forgive your sin?" I knew we had covered this very thing in the previous sessions.

They both nodded yes before I continued.

"Do you want me to pray first and you repeat after me—or do you want to pray yourself?"

"No, no," the girl said, "I got this."

I muffled my spontaneous chuckle so she wouldn't think I was laughing at her. The kid was adorable, and I couldn't help but smile.

Then she prayed, "Lord, I have been thinking about giving You my life for a while now. I've made my decision: You can have me."

With that, she looked up and smiled at me as if she had conquered the world.

All I could say was "Honey, do you want to preach tonight?"

Somehow this child had understood the importance of considering the cost before answering the call of surrendering to Christ. To me, the only explanation for such wisdom was a personal revelation from the Holy Spirit.

A calling begs the question *Am I going to risk everything and say no?* See, to me, that is where the risk lies: in saying *no*, not in saying *yes*. To answer *yes* to God's call is security and blessing (although obedience to Him is anything but a surefire plan for an easy life). Ministry includes the hardships of sacrifice, testing, persecution, and a plethora of other adversities—maybe even death. But there is no greater honor than to work really hard for the Lord. And ministry *is* work; it's hard work, and anyone who tells you otherwise hasn't been in ministry very long, or else they aren't telling you the truth.

That being said, ministry is precious and is required of anyone who has been saved by the blood of Jesus. The Great Commission found in Matthew 28:19 ("Therefore, go and make disciples of all nations.") is not an option; it's a command for each one of His followers.

So as believers in Christ, we're all in ministry. The landscape will look different, the panoramas will vary, and the highways will sprawl in different directions, but He has a mission for each of us. How we live our lives—even in the most ordinary of tasks—can be ministry to those around us. Showing compassion to a frazzled mom waiting in line at the bank or grocery store, giving grace to the oblivious neighbor who mows his lawn at six in the morning, or praying with a friend facing cancer—each situation presents an opportunity to *live* the love of Christ.

When God Called Me

When I was about fourteen years old, I was home alone one day when the doorbell rang. Answering the door, I greeted a church member holding a bottle of wine. It was obvious she had had too much to drink, and she asked to see my parents. I explained they weren't home, but that it would be wise if she came in and waited.

As the clock ticked, she told me her situation of betrayal. Maybe the wine gave her courage to open up to a teenager in a way she wouldn't have if she'd been completely clear minded. Crushed and forsaken, she poured out her heart. Never having experienced that kind of pain, I realized how a broken promise could crumble even the strongest believer. I didn't know anything except that Jesus could heal her heart. All I knew to say was that God loved her very much.

Right then, I realized two things: people's lives are messy, and I wanted to spend my life making disciples. I wanted to be in the chaos of people's lives and to experience God's power to encourage them to surrender. Of course, at the time, I had no idea what that would entail or how hard it would be. But nonetheless, God placed a desire in my heart.

That encounter was sad, simple, and life changing. How did my folks handle the situation? I don't remember what they did or didn't say, and it's not the point. While the rest of the evening is a blur, I know the Lord used a hurting woman to fuel a desire in me to serve Him. People's lives are complex, and ministry is hard, but the bumps along the way tell a story of our relationship with Christ.

What happened to the woman with the wine bottle? Today, decades later, her testimony speaks of God's faithfulness and redemption. Her life has been an example of surrender and salvation, heartache and hope, tears and triumph. As for me, she holds a special place in my heart—and always will.

Marriage? Yuk!

When I was ten years old, my mom suggested that I start praying for my future husband. At ten, I didn't want to *sit* next to a boy, let alone marry one! *Boys have cooties, and they stink.* I remember looking at the kid sitting next to me in school and thinking, *Why doesn't he wash his hands?*

Tommy Blakemore was the first boy who really liked me and showed his affection with a beautiful heart-shaped, sterling silver and turquoise necklace. I was only in sixth grade, and very uncomfortable as he handed me a crumpled plastic bag.

"Here, I got this for you."

Taking it with sweaty palms, I just said, "Thanks."

Then I walked away without opening it. (As it turned out, I really loved the necklace, but lost it a few days later in gym class.)

Even though Tommy was cute and courteous, I couldn't imagine marrying him. At that age, I couldn't imagine marrying anyone! I told my mom I wanted to live with her and Dad forever, so there was simply no need to pray for any man. She just laughed and told me I was welcome as long as I wanted to stay, knowing full well that when independence hit, it would be hard to keep me home. Wise woman, my mother.

I took my mother's advice and started praying for my future husband. At first, my prayers were shallow, simple requests: *May he be good-looking, and please don't let him stink!* But in time, as my relationship with the Lord grew, my prayer life developed as well. It deepened as I prayed for a "man after God's own heart" (1 Samuel 13:14). I prayed that if he were an athlete, he would play fair, winning decently and losing graciously. I asked God to keep him safe and help him make wise choices as he chose friends and activities. Loving music myself, I wondered if he might be a musician, and I asked the Lord to help him practice consistently to develop his talents. I asked the Lord to put a love for travel in his heart. Finally, I requested a man called to full-time ministry—a partner to serve Christ with by building His kingdom.

I also asked the Lord that this mystery man *not* be a pastor. I didn't want to marry a pastor. Missionary, evangelist, youth worker—yes; but not an ordained pastor. For me, the fishbowl life had run its course, and although I desired full-time ministry, the role of pastor's wife sounded like a prison. As wonderful as my childhood was, I wanted other options. My parents did it well, and to this day people comment on their influence, but it was hard. I decided another area of ministry would fit me better.

That's how I prayed, and God graciously blessed me in the middle of instructing Him with what I thought I wanted and what I knew I didn't.

William Tyndale College

During my senior year of high school, I auditioned at William Tyndale College for a traveling public relations music team. My sister Keli, two years older than I and already a student at Tyndale, lived in the dorm at the small Bible college. Tyndale was an interdenominational school and a great local opportunity for both commuters and campus students to receive solid, biblical training for ministry. I remember the day I auditioned for the Tyndale Singers as if it were yesterday.

Looking collegiate in a navy-blue sweater and apple-green slacks, I made my way to the music department. I sang an *Oh, How He Loves You and Me / The Old Rugged Cross* medley in front of the PR team. Dr. Mark White, the music professor and director of the group (who would later stand in our wedding as a groomsman) made me feel comfortable.

Because I loved to sing, it was natural for me to want to attend a college with a good music program, which Tyndale had. But honestly, I'd never thought of myself as talented—only good enough to get by. That's still my perspective. Rarely do I listen to any of our recordings other than to refresh myself with lyrics or harmonies.

When I was in seventh or eighth grade, I overheard a man from my church commenting on the song I had sung in the morning service. "I just don't like her voice—she's not that great," he'd said, and then was shocked to find out I was standing behind him.

Even though those words stung, I agreed. It has taken me thirty-five years to embrace the uniqueness of me. God designed my voice to sound exactly as He intended it to be, and while I enjoy listening to trained singers such as Celine Dion, Josh Groban, or Michael Bublé, the Lord did not give me that kind of ability. Moreover, I never wanted to pursue that type of training. I love telling people about Jesus, and I love worshipping with music; that's it. Period. I'm not trying to *make it* by singing. (Many well-meaning people have told us, "Hang on—one day you'll make it." But I reply, "We *have* made it—right here. Thanks for the compliment, but we're exactly where we're supposed to be. I'm not trying to change the world with my singing; I'm trying to change the world with my worship.")

As I walked into the Tyndale audition room in March of 1986, I had that same attitude: *Just smile and worship the Lord.* And of course, since team members earned a full-ride scholarship, I hoped to make the team.

However, as I entered the room, my eyes fell on a young gentleman sitting at a black baby grand piano. I couldn't tell for sure, but he seemed tall, and his quiet demeanor only added to his good looks. At that moment, I knew he was my future husband. My mind was sure, and my heart reeled. Everything seemed to stop—like in the movies when all action is frozen and the main character has a minute to just observe.

The problem was I didn't have a minute; I had to sing.

Needless to say, I blew the audition; it was just too difficult to focus on my original goal. In an instant, this guy had stolen my heart. So in the end, I didn't get the position, but I did get the pianist. I didn't get the scholarship, but I got the man I prayed for—and he smelled *really* good.

Home for the weekend, my sister greeted me when I walked into the kitchen.

"How did your audition go?"

"Not very well," I said, "but I met him."

"You met who?" she questioned.

Slowly and confidently I said, "I met *him*—the man I'm going to marry!"

Like a good, cynical sister, she continued with the interrogation.

"At William Tyndale College—you met the man you are going to marry? What's his name?" she asked, like I was fabricating the entire story.

"I have no idea!" I said and saw her curiosity piqued. Now I had her attention! After describing him as a good-looking, sandy-blond guy who was probably tall, I mentioned he was sitting at the piano.

She immediately replied, "Oh, that's Randy Brown, my piano teacher. Forget it, girl, you don't have a chance."

Let the games begin.

Because peace accompanied God's revelation, I was able to wait patiently (most of the time, anyway) for God to tell Randy the same thing He'd told me. During my first year at Tyndale, we both dated other people and even double-dated, but we never went out with each other. Actually, it was a great way to get to know him. We laughed more than I ever had and became great friends along the way. One day, sitting in the dorm cafeteria, I announced I was going to the public library a few miles away.

"Anybody coming with me?"

"Sure, I'll go," Randy said, and since we had no other takers, it became the first time we were alone. At the library, I could tell his heart was turning my way, and I saw God working just as He had planned.

After dating seven months, Randy surprised me with a marriage proposal. So I questioned him, "Are you going to be a pastor? Do you sense God calling you to the pastorate in any way? Do you think you will *ever become* a pastor?" (Even though it was the same question, I had to ask it in several ways.)

"No, Marli, I am not called to the pastorate. Full-time ministry—yes. But the pastorate? No."

"Then I will marry you."

Years later, I realized what had happened: I'd prayed for my future husband for so long that when I saw him, I recognized him. We were bound together by a work of the Spirit that comes only through prayer. Have you ever prayed for someone you don't know, and one day realized you hold a deep love for them? That is God's work—doing what only He can do. Because God is love, He can develop love in us for someone we haven't even met. That is why He tells us to pray for our enemies (Luke 6:28).

Prayer is the catalyst that changes our hearts and conforms us to the will of the Father. Prayer connects us to Him who loves us more than we understand. It is one of the disciplines that develops trust and dependence on the Lord in a way which otherwise may never happen. As a little girl, I had no idea that the habit of praying for my husband would become a springboard for talking to God about countless things, from the most insignificant thought to the most important decisions of life. God convinced me that He hears my prayers and answers however He wants.

I wish I'd journaled what and when I prayed for Randy. Had I done that, we could compare my prayers with the specifics of his life. I am certain, from the little I do remember, that we'd be awed by God's answers along the way.

Today, our kids are preparing for their future spouses in much the same way: As Kennedie prays for her future husband, she makes simple notes in a journal recording whatever her heart desires. Every year, on her birthday, she writes him a letter, seals it, and stores it for the future. On her wedding day, the letters will be bound and presented to him so that he can see how God grew this precious girl into a woman of faith by praying for him. Kadison is much more private than Kennedie and, being a boy, will probably prepare differently than his sister. We've prayed for his future wife since the moment we knew he was a boy. Whenever I mention something to consider regarding his wife, he says, "Already prayed about it, Mom." That is the plan, and as best as we can, we are sticking to it. I believe, as parents, we have to be deliberate in our efforts to raise kids who want to know God's plan for their lives. It won't just happen; we have to purpose it.

The great thing is, even if your child is a single adult, you can pray for their potential spouse now. Pray for your grandchildren's spouses, your great-grandchildren's spouses, and every generation to come. Write a letter to leave for your grandchildren's spouses whom you may never meet. Wouldn't it be exciting to receive a letter from your spouse's grandma, describing her prayers for you?

Let's think ahead. With God, it's never too early or too late to pray. He is loving and compassionate, and delights to have His children talk to Him about anything.

The Mystery of Ministry

Randy and I had been married about nine years when he took a position at Shepherd Fellowship Church in Waterford, Michigan, as worship leader and associate pastor.

One day while on staff there, he came to me and said, "Mar, I have to talk to you. I can't shake the feeling. I need to be ordained as a pastor."

Even though Randy was the associate pastor at the church, it was different than being ordained as a pastor. I can't explain it, but to me, it was just different.

"Aw, come on—we had a deal!" I teased. I had to laugh at what God was doing in us, especially in me. Because then, all joking aside, I added, "I know, babe. It's time. Sign up for the classes."

It really was no surprise. I too knew the Lord was calling him to ordination, preparing him for the next level of ministry. In fact, months earlier, I had wondered when Randy would come to me with this news.

He was ordained later that year, in timing that turned out to be critical: soon afterward, our senior pastor died suddenly from a brain aneurysm. It was a tragedy that caught us off guard, but we immediately understood the importance of Randy's ordination. He partnered with the youth pastor and took over responsibilities, such as weddings, funerals, and hospital visits, that required an ordained pastor. We immediately began ministering to the senior pastor's family and to the congregation, who had loved him immensely. It was a year before Randy and I could slow down enough to grieve his death. All of a sudden, we looked at each other and said, "He's gone." Then we grieved.

Through that season of securing Randy's ordination and dealing with our senior pastor's death, God taught me the importance of quick obedience. Deep inside, there was a twinge of pain, considering that I never wanted to marry a pastor. Had I not supported Randy, I could have hindered God's plan, or at least delayed it. God was intentional in His timing, and He placed Randy in an office of responsibility for a specific season. It was important that I be on board. Believe me, I wish I could go back and change my attitude in more situations so God could have accomplished His plans in and through me. But that time—that one critical season—I got it right.

I am thankful God understands our immaturity. He gets our hang-ups and quirks and maneuvers us through things that otherwise would obstruct His plans for us. More than this, He matures us through the issues born out of hurt, pride, and offenses, which need purging. He is patient beyond comprehension and willing to wait for us to align ourselves with His will. Only He can bless us and transform us into His likeness as we fumble through life.

We never thought Randy was going to become a pastor, and we had no idea I would thrive as a pastor's wife. I wasn't mature enough to see beyond my preconceived ideas and petty images, and I was just childish enough to believe that I knew what I wanted. I was wrong. The time we spent on a church staff is something we still treasure today. We learned about handling the pressures of ministry while balancing the pressures of marriage and family life. We gained valuable experience preparing us for future ministry. Now, an important part of our ministry is developing friendships with pastors and their wives across the country. We can relate to hurting pastors because we have been there ourselves.

I am grateful that God took my stubborn heart and softened it to follow His route. If I had gotten my way, I would have missed out on so much.

The Backseat View

It's time to swivel your chair and look at your own life.

Don't worry if this is new to you or if you've not sensed a specific leading by the Holy Spirit. Jeremiah says that God has good plans to prosper us (Jeremiah 29:11), so we know that He has a route mapped for each one of us. Remember: as believers, we are all called to ministry, regardless of whether it's a career or not.

* What has God asked of you specifically?
* Do you sense a call to full-time ministry?
* Are you a disciple of Christ? If so, what has it cost you?

If you have never surrendered to Christ, confessed your sin to God or invited Him into your life and want to do so, take a moment and talk to Him. Like the little girl who went to the altar—why wait? He wants to fill you with His Spirit and clean you from the inside out. There is no better response to His calling than *Yes*.

NO U-TURN

Where Am I?

Geography has never been my thing. I don't mean locating foreign countries; I'm talking about identifying states in our own borders. The only way I could ever remember all fifty states was to sing them. In middle school, I worked tirelessly on a song that listed all the states alphabetically; but today, I can only get through the *I*s. Trust me when I tell you geography is not my strong suit.

My mother-in-law has a natural, God-given love for geography. For Christmas one year, she was presented with the most beautiful marble globe with inlaid gemstones. Randy's dad chose it deliberately because she enjoys searching for a certain country or sea. When she hears of a city or maybe a river that's unfamiliar to her, she immediately studies a map or her globe to find it. And after she finds it, she *remembers* it! It's a satisfying hobby, and she's wired this way. I, however, am not.

One time Randy and I were playing Pictionary (the game where you draw pictures of things and teammates have to guess what they are) with Keli and her husband, Jeff, when my deficiency became abundantly clear: Sitting at their kitchen table, we teamed up boys against girls. When it comes to Pictionary, all of us are very competitive, and the winners enjoy the kill for days to come. That day, Keli and I were thrilled with our strategy and knew the time of our victory was near. I rolled the dice and landed on the geography category. We immediately cried out in the agony of certain defeat.

My heart sank again as I looked at the card and realized my complete ignorance of the US map. I had to draw Illinois. *How did I graduate from college not knowing the location of Illinois?* I wondered. Of course, Randy and Jeff were not about to let us off the hook just because I have a geography handicap. Heartlessly, they turned the small, sand-filled hourglass over as I hastily drew an outline of the country.

"United States!" Keli said with exuberance.

But that was hardly the challenge. The true test was to see how many states my sister could randomly guess within thirty seconds. I took my pencil, shrugged my shoulders, closed my eyes, and randomly stabbed somewhere within the country's borders. Randy and Jeff doubled over laughing and cheered hysterically as I had no idea as to the whereabouts of the Land of Lincoln.

To be honest, I can't remember who won the game—but I'm pretty sure the guys did. Once again, something I should have known but didn't, cost me a victory.

When I was growing up, I could tell you that California is on the West Coast, Florida is south and New York is east. I knew Michigan and Ohio touch and Canada is north, but that was about the extent of my knowledge. I didn't care. It just wasn't important to me to learn the lay of the land. It should have been, but it wasn't. Throughout school, like many students, I learned what I had to for a test, but afterward I immediately forgot the material and failed to commit most of it to long-term memory.

But I wanted to travel. I *loved* to travel. I *needed* to travel, and I prayed that God would let me travel. The thought of growing up and going to the same office every day turned my stomach and made my head hurt. I wanted adventure and experiences, and I wanted to see the places I wasn't even able to locate on a map. I had a deep desire to witness, firsthand, God's incredible creation. I knew it had to be better than the pictures I had seen. Plus, I wanted to set my feet on other soils.

So I prayed consistently that God would include travel in the niche He was carving out for me. Repeatedly, I asked Him to let me build His kingdom while seeing my country. (Kadison got the travel bug as well, but his sights are set on foreign lands like Japan and Spain.) I wanted to go beyond our borders, and I have, but my main desire was to see the United States and experience the different cultures within her.

God said yes.

In His graciousness, God invited me on a journey that included many trips across the country. His plan has been thrilling, as we proclaim the name of Jesus and urge people to repent. Simplicity is the name of the game for us.

As soon as I start comparing our ministry to others, God reminds me to *keep it simple*. We have one mission: to worship with our brothers and sisters in Christ while encouraging the church to repent and remain faithful.

I've had moments when I questioned whether there's enough value in what we're doing. Is there enough fruit for the effort and expense? But then I read about the apostle Paul's mission:

> Traveling through the country, passing from one gathering to another, he gave constant encouragement, lifting their spirits and charging them with fresh hope. (Acts 20:2 *Message*)

Know Your Mission

Paul traveled from church to church, encouraging the believers and reminding them to stay faithful to God. If the church needed it *then*, it definitely needs it *now*. So for many years, Acts 20:2 has been the mission statement for Randy and Marli Ministries.

The New Testament church was greatly in need of encouragement, and Paul was chosen as a mouthpiece of good news and instruction. He spent the latter part of his life building the kingdom of God, but before that, Paul was a Jewish Pharisee—legalistic and rigid.

Of course, the law was given to prove our need for a Savior, but Paul was determined to religiously obey the letter of the law. Prior to believing in Christ as the Messiah, he persecuted and killed Christians in the name of God. Then Paul was supernaturally struck blind on the road to Damascus, when Jesus revealed Himself to him.

Paul used the rest of his time on earth to minister the gospel to people stuck in legalism, sin, feuding, bitterness, rage, and sexual immorality. He had a "heart transplant" and served the Lord fervently. Lives were changed because of God's power working through him. In Galatians 6:14–16, Paul glorified the Lord, saying,

> As for me, may I never boast about anything except the cross of our Lord Jesus Christ. Because of that cross, my interest in this world has been crucified, and the world's interest in me has also died. It doesn't matter whether we have been circumcised or not. What counts is whether we have been transformed into a new creation. May God's peace and mercy be upon all who live by this principle: they are the new people of God.

Because Paul knew his goal, and his purpose had changed, he no longer forced others to keep an impossible law. When God changed his heart, He also changed his mission. Because of this, Paul boasted only in Christ. And in Christ there is a lot to boast about. His work on the cross is all we need to keep us mission minded and focused on evangelizing a hurting world and encouraging a struggling church.

As Randy and I travel from congregation to congregation, we are challenged to believe God more, trust Him more deeply, and follow Him farther. We need to know Him because, like Paul, we minister to weary believers in need of refreshment. God uses situations, mundane activities, ordinary people, tests, trials, and blessings to help us understand His perspective—His love for people. I never could have imagined where my desire to travel and serve God would take me or the incredible servants of Christ I would meet along the way.

The purpose of this book is not to prove the value of our ministry or how many times God speaks to me, but rather to show how God convinced me to follow Him. Much like Paul, it gives me an opportunity to boast in Christ. He led me far beyond my preconceived idea of what I thought my life would look like as God's servant—as a woman, a wife, and a mom. Not only that, but He persuaded me to rely on Him as the driver of my life and ministry. I've learned a lot from the view in the passenger seat.

Kaleidoscope

God cares deeply about the details of my life and is intricately involved in everything from A to Z. I am certain He enjoys my prayers and the time we spend talking about the journey. No, not every prayer has been answered yet, and oftentimes His answers are not what I want to hear. But He is God and doesn't have to explain everything to me. Sometimes though, in a precious moment, He does.

The Holy Spirit has been my devoted teacher, tirelessly coaching me to hear His voice. He taught me the importance of viewing my life by the light of Christ and acknowledging Him as the fuel for everything.

I never understood the purpose of a kaleidoscope, a toy with no use other than viewing patterns of shapes and colors that move when you turn the dial. Never did I want one as a child, nor do I remember having one. If I was given a kaleidoscope in a birthday party goodie bag, among the plastic rings and candy necklaces, it was the first thing I threw out or gave away. As a child, I failed to the see why the simple toy ever became so popular.

But as an adult, I suddenly appreciated its purpose and through it understood something pivotal to my walk with Christ. Depending on where you aim it, the view in the kaleidoscope changes. Pointing it into the darkness, there's nothing to see. However, raising it to the light unveils an unending feast of color and images.

The kaleidoscope suddenly takes on a very different purpose when used this way. Light acts as fuel, and intricate patterns appear. A splendid array of activity materializes, similar to watching a sunrise or sunset. A brand-new scene is yours for the taking as you turn the wheel and witness the effect of light illuminating an otherwise useless object. The shards of broken glass and slivers of mirror inside the kaleidoscope reflect light, resulting in beauty and a vast array of color. The emerging designs inspire me as I discover colors of all sorts: pastels, vibrants, dark hues, and rich tones. Everything changes when I lift the kaleidoscope to the light. The activity and patterns become beautiful with the slightest movement.

That is my life in Christ. When I focus on Him and invite the Holy Spirit to fill me with His light, my perspective changes. I think differently. It's a fresh view, and I find myself hoping for kingdom things instead of earthly ones. Suddenly, I am in line with the will of the Father, and things of the world become less important. With time, my desires turn to pleasing Him instead of satisfying my ungodly passions. When I was saved, I immediately became a new creation, but over time, I'm actually transformed into His likeness, which is the goal.

Without His light and power, I am unable to accomplish anything. In fact, until I realized His love for me, you might say I was one of those shards of broken glass, worthless and useful for nothing. It is He, the *Light* of the World, working in me and through me, that reveals my heavenly design.

The natural result of looking for the Lord is finding Him. It takes time and effort, prayer and sacrifice. But the light of the Holy Spirit is the fuel that runs my life, revealing His love for me—all *while* I seek Him. So the outcome of seeking Him has become a foundation for trusting Him, depending on Him, and without a doubt believing that He is exactly who He claims to be. These blessings have become the colors of my life and the view from my kaleidoscope.

To Homeschool or Not to Homeschool

Here is one example of how God lit my path, changed my view, and gave me a mission.

Homeschooling was never on my bucket list. I had nothing against it; I just didn't want to do it. Granola, candle making, butter churning, homemade soap—none of it appealed to me. Denim skirts weren't my style. I always wondered, *Where do all these homeschoolers buy their jean skirts?* I wanted no part of it.

I soon came to realize what a snob I was. Critical and judgmental were my personal taglines when it came to homeschooling. Why did I have such a strong opinion about something that I actually knew very little about, especially considering I had no personal experience with that specific culture? (And now, after years of homeschooling, I can confidently say it *is* its' own culture.) In fact, my critical spirit was nothing more than a defense mechanism to mask my insecurity. The truth is I didn't think I could do it. Granted, I didn't want to do it, but I really didn't think I could.

Kennedie attended public kindergarten at a wonderful little education center with a loving teacher named Mrs. Widman. She was youthful, smart, and innovative. To this day, Kennedie says Mrs. Widman is her favorite teacher. Please note: she taught Kennedie for one year, I taught her for the remaining twelve—and Mrs. Widman is her favorite! I laugh and thank God for a woman who gave my daughter a really good start. Kindergarten was a great experience, and the graduation ceremony alone was worth the entire year of drop offs and pick ups.

Like most kindergarten teachers, Mrs. Widman regularly incorporated show-and-tell days. Kennedie's turn came, and out of everything she could have taken, she decided on her daddy. She wanted the other kids to see how he played the piano with his whole body. We planned it carefully with Mrs. Widman before the big day finally came.

Kennedie stood in front of her classmates (who were obediently sitting in a circle on floor mats) while Randy inconspicuously leaned against the back wall. Sitting on a child-sized acrylic chair, balancing Kadison and the camera, I was determined to get the whole thing on video. As Kennedie prepared herself to answer questions about her prized possession, she smiled at me and took a deep breath. This, to her, was monumental; she was ready to introduce her dad to her friends and her friends to her dad. One by one, the kids raised their hands with questions to guess the mystery object.

One little boy asked, "Can you hold it?"

Kennedie giggled and said, "Kind of."

"How long have you had it?" someone asked without raising their hand.

"My whole life!" she answered, barely getting the words out as she laughed right from her belly.

The best question was "Where do you put it when you go to sleep?"

The question-and-answer time was just as much fun as the surprise. Finally, Kennedie couldn't hold it in any longer. The classroom was shocked to discover that it was a live person who was Kennedie's show-and-tell mystery item. Then Randy sat down at the piano and played classical, jazz, and country pieces. He was a hit, and Kennedie was a celebrity for the rest of the day.

All that is to say, I loved kindergarten for Kennedie. She excelled, and it provided opportunities I couldn't give her. There was structure, and she formed a bond with Mrs. Widman. It was definitely a great start to her elementary education.

Because the learning center only offered preschool and kindergarten, though, we had to find somewhere else for first grade. We decided to enroll her in the local public school. Later that same day, my mother suggested homeschooling Kennedie.

"Mom, if you want to homeschool my child, go right ahead. I invite you; be my guest. But there's no way I'm homeschooling my kids." (That one statement probably sealed my fate.)

"Would you pray about it for one week?" she asked gently but boldly.

Sighing, I said, "All right, one week. I will pray about it for one week, but don't get excited, Mom."

That night, I said flatly, "Lord, I promised my mother I would pray about homeschooling Kennedie. Here I am, praying about it. Let me know if You want me to do that." I felt a little guilty (but not a lot) about my lack of enthusiasm while praying, but I couldn't muster any excitement whatsoever.

The next day, I began the same way: "Lord, Mom asked me to pray about homeschooling Kennedie, so if You want me to do that ..." and by the time I said *amen*, I felt this excitement soar through my body. My pulse sped up like I was having an adrenaline rush. A shade was lifted from my eyesight, and I saw endless possibilities, like uncharted waters I had never sailed before. In an instant, not only did I *want* to homeschool my child, but I was *excited* to homeschool my child!

Later that night, I told Randy the news.

"Who are you, and what have you done with my wife?" he said in disbelief.

But then, as I told other people about our decision to homeschool, doubt set in. My excitement was squashed; fear and dread overwhelmed me. Several friends said Kennedie should be in the public school system as a light in a dark place. If she wasn't in the public school system, then neither was I, and I wouldn't be able to invest in the community.

How do you feel about that as a believer? Shouldn't you be a witness for Christ in the school system? I became discouraged and confused. I needed more information and direction from both sides. After all, those were valid points worth considering.

I decided to talk with a friend from church who had taught in public school, a Christian school, and for a time had homeschooled her children as well. I didn't know Amy very well, but she seemed like a solid believer, and her kids were *normal*. I met with her to pick her brain, and instantly, Amy saw my dilemma. She described a scenario where you take a tender young plant and strategically place it in a greenhouse:

"A greenhouse is not perfect, but it's the best controlled atmosphere for strengthening that young sapling. You let it grow strong and healthy, all the while watering it, placing it in the sun, and giving it the best nutrients you can. Then, when it's ready, you transplant it outside. You put it out in the natural environment, and because you took the time for it to grow strong, it will have a much better chance of surviving the harsh elements." Then she said, "Marli, no matter how you choose to educate your kids, you'd better be involved."

I will never forget those wise words, and I have passed them on to many young mothers since then. (Years later, I ran into Amy and reminded her of our conversation about homeschooling. She had no recollection of it whatsoever. Isn't it strange how someone can unknowingly make such an impact on your life? It taught me to weigh my words carefully.) But back to my story:

"Where is Kennedie going for first grade?" Mrs. Widman asked me one day while I was collecting Kennedie's backpack and latest art project. I braced myself for another person trying to dissuade me from the road I had set out to travel. She surprised me.

"I think that's wonderful. Do it, Marli. You can give her quality one-on-one time, and she'll do great. It'll be good for her."

I couldn't believe it; a public school teacher was encouraging me to homeschool my daughter! That was the moment of no turning back. It became my "No U-Turn" decision.

The First Day Was Great

Our first day homeschooling went well, but the second day was awful; Kennedie and I both ended up in tears. We hung a calendar on the wall and read some books, which was fun, but all in all, it was a disaster. I was intense and nervous about the future. *What if I ruin my daughter,* I wondered. (Incidentally, it wouldn't be the last time I wondered that.) *As a young girl, I hated school, and now I have to do it all over again.*

We had many days like that during our years of homeschooling, but each year improved. I matured in ways I never would have without homeschooling, and our kids learned the art of self-motivation (which, for our family, does not come naturally). Today, I realize that homeschooling is just as much about the parent as it is about the student. "That seems selfish or unbalanced," you might say. No, not really, because God has the ability to do multiple things at once. Unlike me, He is able to accomplish more than one thing at a time; He is able to make sure the kids are educated while I develop some much-needed discipline.

Little did I know, as God changed my heart for homeschooling, He was setting up our future. In order to travel, we had to homeschool. I didn't calculate that beforehand. God's timing is impeccable, as He always prepares us for our calling. Had He not given me a passion to homeschool, we would have been tied down by the public school schedule.

It became natural to engage in discussions with others about homeschooling as we traveled. Those discussions ranged from curriculum to schedules to frustrations and more.

"How do your kids go to school?" someone would ask, discovering we lived in an RV full time.

"We homeschool," I would reply, anticipating their response. (It didn't take too many years to learn that some regions of the country are much more open to home education than others.)

"Oooohhhh ..." they would say, but it usually sounded much more like *Oh, you're one of those.* Their tone reminded me of my own years before. I became more thick-skinned over time and learned to let people have their opinions while I had mine. It was okay if we didn't agree, and it certainly wasn't my job to change their mind. Homeschooling is not for everyone, but it is a great option.

I enjoy talking about our experience homeschooling—especially teaching the kids to read. It still amazes me that I, only an average reader, taught my children to read! Today's resources are so great that anyone can do it. If you can read, you can homeschool your kid. (Fourth-grade math with its long division, however, is another story and should be left to the professionals. I'm kidding—no, actually, I'm serious. You're gonna need help.)

Socialization

No matter where we are in the country, people ask the same questions and have the same concerns regarding homeschooling. And I understand; as homeschool parents, we deal with these issues continuously (although less so now that we have teenagers). The typical "socialization" issue is always mentioned, as well as patience, discipline, and sheltering.

"How do your children make friends?" is one of the most common questions I get. After all these years (our daughter is now in college, and our son in high school), I don't mind the question. What concerns me is the assumption that public school is necessary for teaching kids how to make friends. *That* troubles me.

I don't mean to overemphasize my point, but think about socialization for a minute—really think about it. Maybe you will come to the same conclusion as I did: everywhere we go, people are there. I have yet to go anywhere in this great land of ours that is, well, *peopleless*. Children learn their socialization skills from their parents, or at least they should. Kennedie and Kadison are observing how Randy and I treat other people, how we respond to and care for others. They may not realize it, but they are learning to interact with others by watching how *we* interact with others. That's a major responsibility for all parents, whether you homeschool or not.

I value friendships, especially lifelong friendships. However, I don't think they are as important as our culture says. By simply reducing the amount of peer influence, our family has avoided many issues that a lot of other families face. Randy and I want to be the ones to mold, challenge, guide, and influence our kids. I shudder as I type this, because we aren't done yet; this is far from over, and they are their own people. We can't control them. But we can control the influences that mold them, at least for a time. When the tender young plant has grown, it will be transplanted and, with God's help, flourish.

It is difficult and even laborious—but not impossible. Wearisome but well worth it. I think it's the personal character issues that make homeschooling such a challenge and to this day, we are addressing some of those same problematic areas in all four of us. After all the praying and pondering, I know three things: we only have one shot at raising our kids, I will never regret our homeschool years, and I couldn't control everything—especially myself.

The Problem Is Me

Living in the RV revealed issues in us. The difficulty for me was *me*. The greatest problem I had with anything was conflict with myself. Whether homeschooling or any other area of my life, I am my biggest problem. Likewise, Randy is his biggest problem, and so on.

Living in an RV was like living in a pressure cooker: whatever is in there will boil to the top (just a whole lot quicker). I didn't struggle with homeschooling because my kids were difficult; I struggled with homeschooling because my lack of patience made it hard. My relationship with Randy had bumps and bruises during those eight years, not because we lived in an RV but because we are two people being molded into one flesh. We weren't agitated as a family because our only home was a camper, but because we were selfish. The RV was merely the pressure cooker God used to bring those flaws to the surface.

Recently, I was in an airport waiting for Kennedie's flight to land. Returning from a two-week trip to Colorado, Kennedie texted me from the tarmac, "We landed. I'm safe, Mom, relax. See you soon!"

In the baggage claim area, I sat in a row of ugly plastic chairs along the window. I was anxious to see her and kept watching the escalator. Knowing it would be a little while before she could deplane and make her way through the airport, I initiated a conversation with the pretty lady sitting two chairs down.

"Who are you waiting for?" I asked.

"My daughter," she answered. "She was in Colorado Springs at a youth conference."

"Mine too!" I exclaimed, realizing they had attended the same event.

Moving to a chair closer to me, she asked, "What do you do?"

"My husband and I have a concert and speaking ministry. We lived in an RV for eight years, traveling the country. We loved it," I told her.

Surprised, she replied, "You're kidding! We're in ministry too. We've always wanted to live in an RV and travel full time. We have *six kids*. Do you think we'd kill each other?"

"Absolutely. And pick out your favorites now because you're gonna lose a few of those kids along the way."

She doubled over in laughter; I was relieved she knew I was joking.

But the truth of the matter is, regardless of *where* we live, we have to monitor *how* we live. House or RV—life in a small area, tripping over one another, can aggravate the most patient person. But that's not the RV's fault. It's mine. It's yours. It's ours.

Our family learned to apologize a lot. We were quick to say "I'm sorry" and quick to forgive. In an RV, there's nowhere to hide, no door to slam to make your point, and very little personal space. We had to learn to live together; to *be* together.

People ask me what it was like to work with my husband full time, homeschool my kids, and live in an RV. Most of the time, the question reminds me that I rarely had a minute to myself, and I instantly start breathing heavy. There was no alone time—no space. We were together 24-7. Day in and day out, we were with each other. It was togetherness, whether we wanted it or not.

But then I think, isn't that why I got married and had kids? To be together?

We needed to learn how to surrender our own agendas and our selfishness. We needed to make room for each other. From the outside, the RV looked big, but after about twenty minutes inside, the walls closed in, forcing me to look out the windshield and focus on the journey. I constantly reminded myself that my life didn't belong to me, and if I wanted to experience God's adventure, I had to let Him drive. I also knew this would give Him time to purge me of anything not pleasing to Him. It was as though He held a mirror in front of my face and said, *This is gonna be a lot more enjoyable if you come with me willingly. Kicking and screaming is only going to make it worse and prolong the process of changing you. I'll get you there, one way or another, but it doesn't have to be miserable. That's your choice.*

His goal for us was to go through those eight years not frustrated, but loving one another in spite of our flaws. Each of us had our own set of issues, and no one sailed through without difficulty. We each handled it differently: a walk around the mall helped me, while Randy needed a couple of hours alone in a bookstore, Kennedie snuggled with our dog, Sammy, and Kadison lost himself in a movie.

Those things helped, of course, but at the very core, we needed to bathe in the Lord's healing Spirit. We learned that you can't merely escape problems but must learn to resolve conflict. The road of relationships can be bumpy, but we have a navigator who knows the terrain and will take the trip with us.

The Joy of Toilet Paper

The bathroom in the RV was small and lacked storage space. There was nowhere to put extra toilet paper, which frustrated me. As a wife and mom, I like a plentiful supply of toilet paper. But in that bathroom, it was impossible. Finally, my frustration peaked and I lost it; I completely blew my cool over bathroom tissue. *Why can't I have a place to store toilet paper, Lord? Aren't I worthy of that? I'm not asking for a house or backyard, just a place to stack some rolls of TP!*

Randy, Mr. Fixit, suggested a solution: "I'll install a thick dowel rod in the corner, behind the toilet. It'll come up from the floor, and you can stack about eight rolls on it."

He got to work addressing this thorn in my flesh and even added a new rug and two wall-mounted storage baskets. When he finished, I was a new girl with a new outlook on life.

Thrilled with my updated bathroom, I got to work reorganizing. I went through the medicine cabinet, discarding old toothpaste and pill bottles, and refolded all the washcloths and towels. I scoured the shower, sink, and toilet, and I cleaned the mirrors. After vacuuming the carpet, I carefully placed the new rug in front of the vanity. Purposefully, I left the brand-new pack of Angel Soft on the couch in the living room until everything was done. Standing back as far as I could in the hallway, I admired my work. The bathroom hadn't been that clean in a while, and it felt great. Finally, the long-anticipated moment came as I stacked each roll on the dowel rod, making a tower of toilet tissue.

Thinking of a totem pole, I squealed, "Hey! Everybody come look at my toilet paper! I love it. Thank you, honey!"

The other three were less than enthused, but it didn't matter; I knew they would be grateful when they needed it.

Just as I was ready to jump in the shower, Randy said, "Now that you're done, I need to dump the tanks. Sorry, you can't shower yet. You'll have to wait; both the gray and the black tanks are full." (That's a polite way of saying the shower and toilet tanks were filled to the brim.)

The RV park where we were staying had only one dumping station, but it was close to our camping site, so I stayed in the bathroom, waiting for Randy to drive to the station. He lined up the dump tank door with the sewer hole and turned off the engine.

"Can you help me?" he said, knocking on the bathroom window from outside. I slid the window open and took the water hose from his hand, pulling it into the bathroom.

"This will be quick—I know you want to shower," he assured me.

I knew exactly what he wanted me to do. After the tank is drained, the person in the bathroom has to aim the hose directly into the toilet (while stepping on the flush pedal in order to open the pipe to the tank) and let the water fill the tank. This gives the tank a good rinse. As gross as it sounds, it's important to rinse the tanks periodically to minimize, well, you know—the odor.

Making sure I had the hose in the right position, I yelled through the window, "Okay; turn the water on!"

I had done this a thousand times. In fact, any one of us could do it, including the kids. But this time, the water shot out like it was coming from a fire hose! The water pressure was so high that I could barely steady the green hose as it danced around like a cobra. There was splashing as the water hit the edge of the seat, and in a split second I realized I was in trouble. The water came out so fast that it immediately filled the toilet tank, and I could see it rising up in the toilet.

With no time to spare, I shouted, "Turn it off—*turn it off!*"

Randy, not knowing the pressure of the water, had gone on to another job at the front of the RV. Hearing my cries for help, he instantly realized what was happening. He made a mad dash to turn off the water, and suddenly everything stopped. I stood there, dripping wet from head to toe, assessing the damage. The walls were dripping, the mirrors were splashed, the freshly folded washcloths were no longer clean, and my new rug was squishy.

But all I could say was "*My toilet paper!*"

Of course it was ruined—the whole stack. My beautiful totem pole of tissue was soaking wet and soggy. And as you know, there's no way to make wet toilet paper usable again.

Randy came running to see if I was okay and burst out laughing.

"How's that toilet paper holder workin' for ya, babe?"

All I'd wanted was a clean stack of toilet paper. Instead I got a shower (and not the kind I needed).

That season of my life didn't allow for some ordinary conveniences, and I quickly learned how petty I could be. Most of us are particular in some sense, but when that fussiness hinders the enjoyment of life, it becomes a problem. Living in the RV, with three other people who had their own peculiarities, I was forced to address some of my petty issues. Some things I could change (although I still love a generous supply of toilet paper, neatly stacked) and some were more of a struggle.

During those years, I realized that my life wouldn't look like other people's. God's plan for me didn't include some of the everyday amenities others had. But it did include many experiences others don't ever get.

If I hadn't viewed my life through His perspective, I could have become discontent and miserable. Instead it was quite the adventure.

Resist the Temptation

It's human to compare. There will always be the temptation to sneak over to a neighbor's property, peer over the fence, and see how they're living. *What do they have that I don't? Are their experiences more exotic? Is life better for them? I wonder if they got that promotion they wanted. I see they're using the brand-name lawn fertilizer. She's really good at geography. Hmm, on their third divorce.*

I really don't mean comparing the kinds of things that we have (although we do that too) as much as comparing how we live. It is normal to compare, but it doesn't have to be our way of life. In fact, it shouldn't be our way of life. Comparison breeds discontentment and envy, or pride. I know because, in one way or another, I experienced all of those.

Wherever we went, people said to me, "I definitely couldn't do what you guys do! I could never live in an RV full time with my family." I would just smile and think to myself, *Well, good—you probably weren't called to live in an RV with your family. So if you did, you'd be disobeying God. Find out what God has called you to, and just do that.*

Because God equips us for what He calls us to, we don't have to worry about comparing ourselves to others. He hasn't equipped me to work in home health care, but he equipped my sister to work in that field. And it's a good thing, because she has ministered to families I will never meet. I don't have the equipping—or the stomach—for that calling. But she does because He equipped her. Without the equipping, she wouldn't be successful in her position.

His equipping comes with more than just tangible things such as money or an RV; it comes with vision, patience, and ability.

> May He equip you with all you need for doing His will. May He produce in you, through the power of Jesus Christ, every good thing that is pleasing to Him. All glory to Him forever and ever! Amen. (Hebrews 13:21)

The Backseat View

Regardless of what the issue is, whenever I ask the Lord to give me a new perspective—to view my life through His light—the stress, pressure, and anxiety vanishes. In many ways, God used a camper to alleviate unnecessary burdens. Those were very freeing years, and the lessons from them have changed me forever. I am glad too because I needed to change. I want to change, and my family *still* wants me to change. (I want them to change too, but that's a different book.) Here is the point: Each of us has to ask the Lord what He has for us. *What is Your will for me, Lord, and how are You going to get me there?*

Maybe you feel lost and don't have a clue where you are. Maybe your geography skills leave a little to be desired and this season of your life is confusing. Your mission may be unclear. You might need to let the Lord transform your mind so you can discern His will. You may never have considered the view through His kaleidoscope, or yours may be completely dark. If so, there could be some character issues clouding your view.

So swivel your chair and look inward:

* Have you experienced the filling of God's Spirit, and do others see patterns of faithfulness in your life?
* What character issues do you struggle to conquer?
* What petty quirks steal your joy?
* Has comparison become a trap for you?
* Do you feel lost, without a map?
* What is God's will for you?

Whenever I've lost my way, can't seem to focus, or just have a meltdown, I cry out and ask God to rescue me. Take a personal moment and talk to Him about whatever is on your heart.

Our 1994 Thor Ambassador at the Great
Salt Lake (Salt Lake City, Utah.)

Looking into the galley of the RV, with the bunks on the left.

The captain's chairs of the RV.

The RV parked in a gorgeous campsite.

Randy doing his least favorite job: dumping the tanks.

The RV on a hoist for repair work. Randy always stayed close
by to make sure they were going as fast as possible.

Kadison and Sammy watching a movie in his "Giant Cat Box."

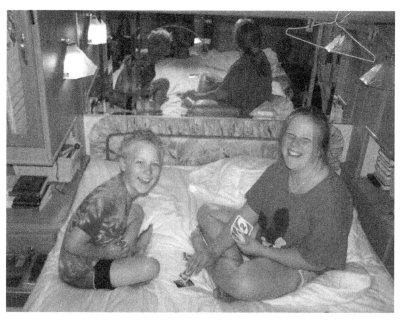

Kennedie and Kadison traveled thousands of miles
while playing games in the back bedroom.

The RV decorated for one of many birthdays celebrated in the RV. This picture gives a good idea of the actual living space.

Randy calling pastors to book concerts. It was challenging to stay quiet for hours while he was on the phone.

Randy giving Kadison a piano lesson on the back bed.

Kennedie, Sammy, and Kadison homeschooling in the RV.

Sammy with his paws on the steering wheel.

Kennedie and Kadison doing homework while waiting for the RV to be fixed. The kids did homework at a lot of repair shops across the country.

Randy and Kadison changing a tire on the trailer.

Christmas in Palmdale, California, with my entire family. (L to R: My dad, Marv; Amber; my mom, Shirley; Kadison; Jeff; Kennedie; Keli; Kierstin; myself; Celeste; and Randy.)

Kennedie with my geography buff mother-in-law, Glenda, and father-in-law, Ron, who prayed daily for our RV from bumper to bumper.

The cousins, who frequently traveled with us. (L to R: Amber, Kierstin, Celeste on Kennedie's lap, and Kadison in the back.)

Kennedie and Kadison at Cracker Barrel, when they had no idea where we were in the United States.

Kennedie and Kadison imitating Randy and me in a talent show. The crowd loved it; those two were spot-on.

GPS (GOD PLANNED SOMETHING)

Homesickness

I have always struggled with homesickness. Sometimes during our eight years of living in the RV, I experienced that same kind of feeling, even when I had no home to be sick *for*. It was the strangest sensation, and I couldn't explain it, but I longed for a place that didn't exist—at that moment, anyway.

Back when I was in high school, I quit cheerleading because the whole team had to go to a weeklong cheer camp. There was no way I was going, and no one could convince me to go. It was too far away and for too long, and my mom couldn't go with me. I simply wasn't brave enough to leave the familiar and experience the unknown. Little did I know, my dream would break me out of my comfort zone and stretch me far beyond my little bubble.

I know it's silly, but all the while I dreamt of traveling, I never connected it with leaving home. I never considered drivers and passenger seats and fuel prices. I didn't think about speaking or writing or even recording. I was void of specifics, but I knew I wanted to do something out of the ordinary. I knew I didn't want to go to the same office every day and do the same thing.

There was no way I could have known exactly what God was planning, and I left the details to Him. But I did pray about it—a lot. I asked the Lord to direct and plan something for me that I couldn't imagine. He did. I had a dream, and so did Randy. God placed a dream inside both of us, and together, we discovered it.

We went to Disney World on our honeymoon, and right there in the middle of Magic Kingdom, I burst into tears.

"What's wrong, Mar?" Randy asked, wondering what he'd gotten himself into.

"I miss my home. I love you, but I've got this lonely feeling. I don't understand it, but I feel homesick."

He was eating a blueberry crepe and offered me some, "Well, want a bite?"

I don't think he knew what to do. But he put his arms around me and loved me through it. It wasn't the first time I'd cried about leaving home, and it wouldn't be the last.

Ten days later, returning from our honeymoon, we loaded his car with my luggage and our wedding gifts and began the five-hour drive from my parents' house to our upper flat in Cincinnati, Ohio. As I took one last look around, tears began to roll down my cheeks. I clung to the doorknob. Randy pried my fingers off and said, "Come on. Time to go."

I sobbed all the way to Toledo. "I … I … I … love you, and I really want to be married to you—I just miss my family."

Finally I calmed down and tried to enjoy the rest of the trip. When we got to the apartment (where Randy had already lived for a year), I immediately noticed the living room walls; he'd hung posters everywhere with messages like *Welcome Home, Marli* and *I Love My Wife*. It was very romantic and thoughtful. Then I entered the kitchen, which, on the contrary, wasn't romantic and thoughtful. Every dish Randy owned was on the counter or in the sink—dirty. He had covered them with towels, maybe to keep the mice and cockroaches away, or maybe so I wouldn't notice. But I did, and the first thing I had to do in my new home was wash every dish it contained. That was just a precursor to motherhood. Funny it didn't bother me. (Well, I just told you about it—so obviously, it didn't go away either.) To this day, Randy says, "I can't believe I did that." Eh, no biggie, it gave me something to do and a great story to tell.

I enjoyed unpacking my things and setting up the flat just the way I wanted. I'm glad I married young, because I was too ignorant to understand what a life change it really was. Only five months removed from the status of teenager, I was much more flexible with my life. It was simply preparation for a life of constant change and motion. New people, new places, and an unknown calling were waiting for me.

Looking back, I see that I never realized how my homesickness could have gotten in the way of my calling. Something that for a time ruled my life could have derailed me, steering me to an alternate course. But God gave me a partner who made sure that didn't happen—a man who desired to follow God even more than I did. Together, we tackled some of our most personal issues—issues Satan meant for harm, to divert us. Homesickness was just one of those. I would have missed out on an amazing ride if I'd allowed the love of home to keep me there.

Say It Out Loud

For several years, Randy and I struggled with where we were in life— compared to where we wanted to be. Married for fourteen years and serving on a church staff, we did concerts on the side. The desire for a full-time concert ministry grew until we could no longer ignore its pull.

Lying in bed talking one night, I simply asked him, "Honey, if you could do anything—don't think about money or the kids or the house or debt or the dog, just about you—what would it be?" I just wanted him to say it.

He thought silently for what seemed like ages. When he did speak, he tripped over his words and stuttered. He and I both knew the answer, but he needed to say it—out loud.

Finally I sat up, looked him right in the eyes, and said, "It's okay. Say it."

He took a breath and said, "I want to be in a worship concert ministry and travel the country."

"Good. Me too."

With that, the tides changed, and we had a new mission. Not only were we reading the same book, but we were on the same page. Our hearts were in unison as God was mapping His route for us.

Immediately, we took stock of where we stood. We worried that people would think we had an unrealistic perception of our talent. If you know us at all, hopefully you've seen this couldn't be further from the truth. In fact, it has taken me years to write this book simply because I was convinced I had nothing to say. And besides that—someone else should say it.

But that night, we remembered what our favorite college professor, Dr. Gordon Ainsworth, had drilled into our impressionable young minds: *God formulates a dream in your heart; don't let it die.* He constantly told us to love Jesus, work hard, keep the dream alive, and trust God to get you there. We definitely had a dream in our hearts, and that night, we named it. To some, our dream might have seemed simple; to others, complex. But that didn't matter, because it was given to us.

Most believers know Psalm 37:4: "Delight yourself in the Lord and He will give you the desires of your heart." Over the years, I have found this to be true, but my understanding of it has changed. I used to think it meant that God gives us what we desire because our heart aligns with His will as we draw near to Him. But now, I think He actually places a specific desire in our heart. Maybe it's both. But I do think He puts a dream in our hearts in order to accomplish His plan through us. Then, according to His timeline and our obedience, He grants the desire.

It could be that the passion you are stifling is the seed God has planted in your heart, and now He's growing it. It takes time to cultivate a dream and let it mature into fruition. Your heart is the soil, which must be tilled and prepared for growth and change.

For me, that happened with maturity. Maturity brings understanding, and with understanding comes patience. We had to learn to wait for God's timing. Timing is vital in His plan, and sometimes our lack of patience disrupts our obedience. I've noticed that God is in no rush—but I am. While there is nothing I can do to hurry Him along, there is, however, much I can do to prepare for His appointments. That gives me plenty to do while waiting for Him to determine my steps.

> We can make our plans, but the Lord determines our steps. (Proverbs 16:9)

Once Randy finally voiced his dream, we could move on. Until then, we were on hold. We had a passion for traveling in a concert ministry and couldn't shake it. When Randy finally named our dream, only then did we realize it was the seed God had planted in our hearts. Why did we think our dream was not from God? Why did we get sidetracked, thinking the very thing we were excited about was not from the Lord? We were so passionate to serve Him in concert ministry that it almost seemed too good to be true.

I have found it has a lot to do with wiring. We are all wired differently, and what thrills you may not be that thrilling to me—and vice versa. God has such variety in His creation that we can't expect to all want the same things. If we all had the same passions, very little ministry would be accomplished, and needs would be unmet. Randy and I were wired for this nomadic lifestyle because God wanted us to *go*.

He calls some of us to travel and encourage the body of Christ, to feed the sheep. With the wiring, passion, and calling—comes the equipping. So then, He readied us. We met two kinds of people during our RV years: those who ached to do the same thing and those who felt sorry for us. Rarely were there any in between.

Of course, we couldn't begin a concert ministry the night Randy voiced our dream, but we certainly found the starting line. In scripture, we often see that a time of preparation follows a calling. God used that waiting period to prepare us. Our marching orders sounded a lot like "Hurry up and wait." But while we waited, we fasted and prayed—a lot.

There were tons of questions with no easy answers, and the *hows* overwhelmed me. Our faith was stretched, and new muscles of trust were developed. Good thing, too, because we've needed those muscles to carry us through tough situations and trials. Those testings strengthened us and showed us God's great care for us.

We had to develop patience and wait for God's timing. Waiting on God was anything but easy—but neither was it a waste of time. He used that time well in our lives. In fact, it produced character, perseverance, and strength (see Isaiah 40:31). In the coming years, we would need every one of those godly attributes to live together without killing each other.

How Do I Know God's Will?

That's a great question, and I'm glad you asked it. One of the most common questions believers ask is "How can I truly know God's will for my life?" Romans 12:2 says,

> Do not conform any longer to the pattern of this world,
> but be transformed by the renewing of your mind. Then
> you will be able to test and approve what God's will is,
> His good, pleasing and perfect will.

I learned this verse as a high school Bible quizzer, and it seeped into my soul. Thirty years later, I am still discovering what it means to "not conform." To know God's will, we've got to grapple with what that means. If we don't, discerning His will is going to be nearly impossible. Why? Because His will rarely mirrors what the world thinks our lives should look like.

Dictionary.com defines *conform* this way: "To act in accordance with the prevailing standards, attitudes, practices, etc., of society or a group." That explains it well. When we conform, we join the world's way of thinking. Unfortunately, society as a whole rarely takes into consideration God's idea of holiness, purpose, value, or calling. If we conform to the world, we will miss His will.

God tells us to guard against blending in with the world, allowing our minds to be polluted. Instead, He wants to change (or transform) our minds with His righteousness.

How does that happen? It's obvious, right? Absorb God's Word. Read it, study it, devour it. Tuck it into our hearts and let it spill out of our mouths. That, right there, will change the course of our lives because, according to God's promise, we will know His will.

The only way for our mind to be renewed or restored is to read the *truth*. God revealed Jesus to us in His Word, and believing Him will refresh, regenerate, rehabilitate, and make our minds new. I must pursue Jesus (*the* Truth) with all that I am. And while doing so, God helps me stand on His promises instead of conforming to the pattern of the world.

Lives lived this way will look different, and they should, because very few things in society reflect the glory of God. But we were created to look like Him. We can know His plans for us and enjoy a life with ultimate purpose. He designed it that way.

We must pursue truth without conforming to the world. However, as believers, we seem to have mastered the art of conformity. Because the world has influenced so much of the church at large, unbelievers see very little difference in us. We look just like them. Our lives aren't all that different. So not only do we struggle to discern God's will, but we end up making no difference at all. But with a mind filled with truth, and transformed by the power of God, we will know His plans for us and affect others as we live out our calling.

When we allow Him to change us, life becomes purposeful and passionate, fulfilling His desires for us. We have found no greater satisfaction than to be in the center of His will.

It's not easy. Life is hard, and we struggle—Jesus said we would, so that's to be expected. But could it be that as twenty-first-century Christians, because we don't resist the pull of the world and we're so comfortable with sin, our minds haven't been renewed, and discovering God's will has become nearly impossible? I believe this is why so many of us struggle to know what He wants us to do in life. We can't think past the junk that fills our thoughts. It's imperative to surrender every thought, want, and habit to the only One who can actually change us.

Even when I focus on God's Word and allow Him to wash my thoughts, discernment takes time. It also takes courage. You might think, *I think God is telling me to ...* or *God put this on my heart.* But the only way to know for sure is to walk that way. Walk toward the vision and obey as best you can. Is it easy? Not for me. But this is a vital part of our relationship with God—being completely dependent on Him. He is the God of patience, trial and error, and redemption. *Blessed* redemption.

Colossal Mistake

During our first concert ministry tour, we spent two months in Florida. As a brand-new, love-offering, faith-based ministry, our resilience was shaky at best. Right from the start, we seemed to face one test after another.

Thousands of miles from home, I took a walk through a subdivision lined with trees covered in Spanish moss. Alone and watching for falling spiders and dangling snakes, I suddenly thought, *What in the world are we doing with our lives, and what if we've made a terrible error? Is this really God's will for us?* My emotions welled up, and tears began to fall. I started to feel that familiar ache of homesickness. No longer was I concerned about spider bites or venomous serpents; I was scared to death that we were making irreversible decisions.

I poured my heart out to God, questioning every decision we made that had landed us where we were that day. With few concerts, little money, and a bag full of doubts, I rambled. I opened up a storage shed full of emotion and invited Him in. All of my thoughts narrowed down to one question: *Lord, what if we're making a colossal mistake?*

God answered me in that moment with unmistakable clarity: "Marli, with Me, what's a colossal mistake? What can you do that I cannot redeem?"

End of discussion. I stopped walking, stood in the middle of the sidewalk, and looked up into the sky—a vibrant ocean-blue, the puffy white clouds almost seeming misplaced. I felt like God was close enough to hug. He was walking with me and in me, before me and behind me. He surrounded me. I enjoyed the rest of the walk, crying, but with tears of gratefulness, peace, and confidence. No longer were spiders or snakes on my mind. A much broader picture had emerged: The dream we treasured, our passion, the desire of our heart, God's will for us—all of this was to be *enjoyed*. Walking with Him, we weren't to fear anything.

Were there things to fear? Of course; there always will be. Homesickness, fear, doubt, or any other device of Satan will steal your joy and your calling—if you cave in to it. So stand strong and believe the truth.

Lola

I would be a rich woman if I had a dollar for every time someone asked me, "Have you seen the movie *RV*?"

"Not only have I seen it; I lived it," I say, laughing.

The four of us saw it together in the theater while munching on popcorn and Junior Mints. We loved it and eventually bought it, adding it to our DVD collection. Because it hits so close to home, we quoted it constantly. My favorite line came from the mom at the end of the film, when Carl (the son) offers a solution to the family's financial woes.

"We could all live in the big rollin' turd and be homeschooled!"

"That just sounds *fantastic*," says the mom sarcastically. In the theater, we exploded with laughter and applauded, giving the other moviegoers quite a shock. I am sure they wondered why that line elicited such an outburst from us.

Robin Williams was hilarious talking to his GPS, which he named Lola. So we named our GPS Lola. We tried switching the voice mode to a British or hipster accent, but it just didn't work. We missed Lola and went back to the familiar voice telling us where to go.

Sometimes Randy gets mad at Lola because she leads him to nowhere land. We are constantly driving to places we have never been, so our GPS is always with us. We punch in the address, and she speaks the directions. But sometimes, we end up at an empty field or condemned building. Then

Randy scolds her, "Aw, come on, Lola, what are ya doin' here? You're killin' me." He resets her, and she recalculates.

It usually works, but it frustrates my husband because he feels mocked. She says, "Recalculating," but to him, it sounds more like "You're an idiot because you didn't follow directions the first time, and now you have to turn around." He continues the conversation with her, "Lola, I only went where you told me to go. Don't get sassy with me."

I remain calm and remind him, "Randy, you know she's not real, right?"

He replies, "Shhh. She can hear you."

The best thing about our GPS is the Home button. When we bought a house after our eight years of RV life, the first thing Randy did was program Lola with our home address. Now, no matter where we are in the country, he can click Home and she tells us how to get there. It doesn't matter whether we are in Canada or Mexico, Lola routes our course and leads us to our driveway. She even tells us the exact minutes it will take and the number of miles we have to drive. Now that we own a house, it is comforting to know our GPS will always get us there.

I Will Show You Where to Go

While living in the RV, I studied Genesis 12:1–5, which details God's call to Abram (later renamed Abraham):

> The Lord had said to Abram, "Leave your native country, your relatives, and your father's family, and go to the land that I will show you. I will make you into a great nation. I will bless you and make you famous, and you will be a blessing to others. I will bless those who bless you and curse those who treat you with contempt. All the families on earth will be blessed through you." So Abram departed as the Lord had instructed, and Lot went

with him. Abram was seventy-five years old when he left Haran. He took his wife, Sarai, his nephew Lot, and all his wealth—his livestock and all the people he had taken into his household at Haran—and headed for the land of Canaan.

Since Abram didn't know where God was taking him, I could relate. On a smaller scale, I understood the excitement of following God's plan while aching with every goodbye. Abram didn't cling to his native country or beg to stay near family, and neither could I. He didn't convince everyone to go with him. He simply obeyed. But I bet it wasn't simple at all. I think it was probably scary and hard and uncomfortable. I am sure it was inconvenient and unfamiliar. Nonetheless, he went.

Over the years, people have told me their views about moving far from family. Many people have said that extended families are meant to stay together, living close to one another. I understand too because most of us want to be in close proximity in order to help each other. That is practical, good, and loving.

In fact, that's why I studied this passage in the first place. Several people questioned me about leaving our families. They were kind but determined, and it caused me to doubt. Then I remembered that Abram was asked to leave his family and home. I was too. A calling can take you away from family and the familiar. During that time of starting out in the RV, this passage was a source of encouragement to me. I missed my family and dealt with homesickness on a regular basis, but I knew we were in the center of God's will. "We are home, we are home," I would say in moments of homesickness.

The thing is, when we left, life continued as normal for everyone who stayed. Things changed: friends and family got married, people died, babies were born, kids graduated. We missed a lot. We couldn't get back for every funeral or make it to every wedding. Holidays were compromised while the clock just kept ticking. When we finally did make it home to see family and friends, they too had changed. Things weren't the same as when we left, and ironically, I felt left behind.

It was nothing anyone did, and it certainly wasn't anyone's fault. It was just life moving along. It wasn't something we could have foreseen or even prevented; we just had to weather it. God asked us to adjust to changing relationships, and He helped us make that adjustment. He made us feel welcome in our own lives, our own calling. He made me feel comfortable, while I found my home in Him.

Home

Those initial feelings of insecurity forced me to consider what a home is and what it isn't. As a citizen of heaven, I take great comfort in Paul's words in Philippians 3:20:

> But we are citizens of heaven, where the Lord Jesus Christ
> lives. And we are eagerly waiting for Him to return as
> our Savior.

This means I am not to consider this earth my home, but rather, heaven. I shouldn't get so entangled in the trap of feeling comfortable or welcomed here that I forget where my true home is. Nothing on earth should feel completely like home, because we are just travelers passing through. Our time on earth is short, and until God completely restores heaven and earth, it shouldn't feel totally like home.

That's the story behind the song "I Am Home" from our album titled *Home*. I wrote the lyrics while living in the RV:

> Lost in a dream, of where I should be, remembering I
> am Yours
> Hoping to find a place all my own, familiar, safe and secure
> I can't describe the way that I'm feeling, confident I am
> where I belong
> All that I have is in Your safe-keeping
> You write my story, I'll sing Your song

Cradled by love, I am home, safe in Your arms, not alone
No matter where the road is leading, feels like going home
If You're there, If You're there, I am home

Tossed by the waves, of doubt and despair, trusting in
Who I can't see
You lead the way, content I will be, following Your plan for me
I can't describe the way that I'm feeling, confident I am
where I belong
All that I have is in Your safe-keeping
You write my story, I'll sing Your song

Cradled by love, I am home, safe in Your arms, not alone
No matter where the road is leading, feels like going home
If You're there, If You're there, no matter where
If You're there, If You're there, I am home

The Backseat View

It's time to swivel your chair and take a look at yourself. If you've been doing that all along—great. But if not, take a few minutes now and evaluate yourself. It helps to take stock and ask questions:

*   Do you struggle with feeling at home in your own life?
*   Is the pull of the world so enticing that you are unable to discern God's will?
*   What desires has He placed in your heart?
*   Does your passion and wiring line up with God's will?
*   Do you wish you had a personal GPS to recalculate your route and point you in the right direction?
*   Has God given you a mission that doesn't resemble anything you have ever known?

* Are you in the process of preparation for your calling?
* Are you patiently waiting for God's timing?
* Have you made mistakes that you don't think God can redeem?
* Do you consider heaven your home?

One day we stopped at a restaurant for lunch. The kids were engrossed in a game and still in their pajamas. Randy and I stretched our legs in the parking lot while we waited for them to get dressed.

Jumping out of the RV, Kennedie said, "Where are we?"

"Cracker Barrel," I shot back, knowing they loved the pancakes.

Kadison spoke up: "No, like, where are we in the *United States*?"

They had no clue—neither one of them. We could have been in Maine or Montana, California or Connecticut; they didn't know.

Sometimes, life feels like that to me. God leads me somewhere, to someone or something, and I have no idea why. I don't recognize anything, and I can't figure out where I am. Discernment seems to escape me, and I can't remember my mission.

There have been moments when I've fallen to my knees and questioned everything He has led me to. But time and again, God revives the dream in my heart and reminds me of what He has done in my life. It is so grand, I can't ignore it. He is the ultimate navigational system, and He recalculates my route with each wrong turn. God doesn't get flustered, He never needs to be reset nor will He ever direct me to a dead end. His path always leads me home.

CONSTRUCTION ZONE

I Hate Camping

I am pure sanguine. If you're familiar with the four personality types (the other three are melancholic, phlegmatic, and choleric), you know that sanguines love to have fun. In fact, we *live* to have fun. For a true sanguine, boredom is death. To quote my husband: "My wife can have a party all by herself."

During our engagement, I had a bit of a meltdown wondering what I would do with my free time after we were married. To reassure me, Randy reminded me that I had to finish the last two years of my college education. As if that wasn't enough, he suggested an additional option: if I was still bored, I could get a part-time job. And of course we would be involved at church. Sensing that I still wasn't convinced that life would be fun, he simply said, "Oh, we can throw a party."

That was all I needed.

So I am sanguine, but I am not a camper—I don't *camp*. I never have, or ever will, enjoy camping. When I think of camping, I think of rainstorms and bugs and grit. Sand in the bedsheets and the dampness from rain and humidity make me miserable. I hate camping.

One time when I was young, we went camping and I walked barefoot over a pile of hot coals from a barbecue someone had dumped by the side of the road. I'd thought they were just rocks. Needless to say, my feet blistered severely, and I spent the week on my back.

The last time I camped as a child, we were caught in a hailstorm. My mother (who is even less of a camper than I) was sitting on the bed in the pop-up camper, trying to weather the storm, when a huge piece of hail hit her on top of the head through the canvas cover. Although Keli and I were doubled over with laughter, it was not as funny to her. "That's it! Marv, get me to a hotel right now!" said my mother, who was usually up for any adventure. Within minutes, we were in the station wagon, luggage and all, headed for the nearest Holiday Inn. We never camped again.

While living in the RV, Kennedie and Kadison often asked if we could go camping. I would just stare at them in utter confusion, not knowing what to say. I didn't even know where to begin with that request. After all, for at least a year, they'd slept in sleeping bags on a hide-a-bed couch, side by side, in a *camper*. Every night we "flattened" the couch (actually it tilted to one side) and arranged the sleeping bags. In the morning, we rolled them up and stored them. I figured that was enough camping for anyone. Oh man, even as I type this, I am reliving it, and it just sounds miserable—the mess, the inconvenience, and no bed for my kids. The constant feeling of just making do; everything seemed *temporary*. Those first couple of years were especially challenging as we learned how to flex.

After living in the RV for about two years, we realized we had to make the living area more usable, so we removed the table and chairs and added bunk beds instead. That way, both of the kids could have their own space. We covered the newly constructed plywood walls in carpet (thus making them resemble huge cat boxes). Pleated shades were affixed to the opening, so they could have complete privacy. They had their most prized possessions tucked into their bunks, with flip-down DVD players and headphones and new bedding. Kennedie had a fluffy, bright pink blanket with multicolored hearts all over the sheets. Kadison's bedding was from the Pixar movie *Cars*, which was all the rage at the time. It worked perfectly, and even though I missed having a table where we could all sit down, it was well worth it.

A few years later, Kennedie (who inherited Randy's height) began to consistently complain of lower back pain. It wasn't until then that I realized she had grown so tall that straightening her legs in the bunk was impossible. Unbeknownst to us, for months she slept with her knees bent. Randy immediately found a solution: With the help of a Sawzall, he cut a hole in the end of her bunk so she could stick her feet out and straighten her legs. Kennedie was overjoyed and repeatedly thanked him for fixing the problem. Sometimes, we hung a towel on her feet as a joke. My heart rejoiced and broke at the same time.

As she grew taller still, we eventually turned Kennedie's bunk into a storage area and moved her back to the pullout couch. She had no choice, and yet she never complained. That taught me something. Her response taught me to take change in stride and learn to adapt. Unknowingly, she helped me see the positive instead of focusing on what I no longer had. She probably never realized how her example challenged me. I'm not sure I realized it either, but looking back, both Kennedie and Kadison helped me to adapt by the way they adjusted day by day. They went with the flow, and I realized that if my kids could do it, then so could I.

I Don't Think You Realize Just How Much I Hate Camping

One of the reasons camping is so rough for me is because I don't like coolers. Have you ever noticed the stale smell of a cooler when you open it? Regardless of what's in it (or even if it's empty), there is this odor that comes wafting out. I *do not* like that. When you camp, you put your food in a cooler and fill it with ice to keep things cold. Then the ice melts, and whatever is in there gets wet and soggy, no matter how expensive your Ziplock bags are. Wet bologna turns my stomach, and I refuse to eat potato salad that's been sitting in six inches of melted ice.

One time, we were headed to Southern California and stopped to see my aunt and uncle in Atlanta. Giving them a quick tour of the RV, we noticed that our refrigerator had died. Just like that; all of a sudden, it didn't work.

Uncle Guy ran to a nearby store and bought us the nicest cooler on wheels he could find. We filled the cooler with ice and the food from the fridge. Everything fit, and it sat in the living room right next to the couch.

Aunt Jeanne said, "Well, now you're really campin'!"

"Yes, this feels dangerously close to camping," I said.

We laughed and thanked them for the cooler. The minute we got to Southern California, we found an RV shop and scoped out a new refrigerator. It was over sixteen hundred dollars for the model we needed. Instantly I thought, *Come on, it's like half the size of a normal fridge!* Owning an RV is not cheap. I guess they figure if you can afford the payment, you can afford the repairs.

Because there was only one model that would fit, we had no choice. But we didn't have two nickels to rub together, let alone sixteen hundred dollars. So while we waited for God to supply a new fridge, the cooler stayed in the living room and doubled as another chair while it held our food. I was discouraged and wondered how we were going to come up with the money for that repair.

Several days later, we led worship for a weeklong revival at a Nazarene church in Chula Vista. The pastor asked to see the inside of our RV, which was a very rare request. He sat down, and we chatted for a while.

Noticing the cooler, he asked, "What's *that* for?"

"Our fridge died, so we are making do," Randy said.

"Why haven't you replaced it?" he asked.

"Well," Randy continued, a bit sheepishly, "it's sixteen hundred bucks for a new one, and right now, we just don't have it."

"Oh ..." was his only response.

I specifically remember the people from that revival. They were so loving! It was a small church, but every night the services were packed. During the final service, we thanked God for what He had done in all of us that week.

The pastor stood before his congregation and said, "Listen, folks, Randy and Marli are servants of the Lord who live in a camper. I was in that camper and noticed a cooler. I asked what it was for, and they told me their fridge had died. It's sixteen hundred dollars to fix it, and I think we should all chip in and pay for it. But here's the thing: if we just give them the money for the fridge, they have nothing to live on for the rest of the week. So let's see what God does."

We were sitting on the front row, and I began to thank God for whatever He was going to do.

The offering was over three thousand dollars.

In an instant, camping didn't seem like such a big deal.

Stuff

Another reason I don't like camping is because of all the stuff you have to lug. (I can hear a minimalist saying, "If you only take what you need, it's easy." Yeah, right. Tried that. Still hate it.)

Like most other Americans, we have a lot of *stuff*. My continuous conundrum was how to make more room in the RV. With all of our personal belongings, homeschool curriculum, remote ministry office, keyboard, guitars, toys, and piles of dirty laundry, of course it felt cluttered. It could have been less cluttered if we had been willing to live without some things we thought were necessities, but we weren't. If I ever have the opportunity to live in an RV again, I will do it with less—much less. Things tend to weigh you down, literally. We hauled all of that stuff for tens of thousands of miles. I'm not sure it was necessary.

One day, I cleaned out the kids' closets. They each had a small cupboard, one foot by three feet. They were located on either side of the queen bed in the master suite. As I emptied Kadison's closet, I found about fifty rocks he had collected all along the way. I couldn't believe it. We had no clue. Quietly, this kid had picked up rocks from all over the United States and stored them in his private space. Big rocks, little rocks, pretty ones, and ugly ones. Some were smooth, some were rough, and some still had dirt on them. He'd built a personal rock quarry right above my head, and I had no idea. And we'd lugged them with us for who knows how long. Yeah, we had stuff.

When I consider how most of the world lives, I realize we actually had a lot of space. But compared to how we were used to living, it was cramped. And since we were constantly changing locations, it was transient. Nothing seemed constant, and just when I thought I was fully adjusted, things would change. One minute I felt great, and the next minute I thought I might just lose my mind. Eventually, I trained myself to quit looking for consistency. I convinced myself to trust the Lord as I transitioned to each season as it came. It was hard, but over time, I learned to be more flexible.

Agility Doesn't Come Naturally

Flexibility is a must for everyone who wants to know God. To have an intimate relationship with Jesus, we must flex and bend as He directs. It's a conscious decision we have to make. If we're not careful, we might just dig our heels in to hold our ground. Without knowing it, we'll stick to our guns and do what we've always done. Status quo.

Life then becomes a rut, and we get stuck trudging along the same path, doing the same thing. Even if God is leading us elsewhere, we'll keep the same patterns simply because we lack flexibility. Living in the RV provided me with the opportunity to learn flexibility in my marriage, with my kids, and in our ministry.

Long ago, Randy and I decided that one of our goals was to raise godly children who believe the Word of God and stand as warriors. That has not and will not change. It is our goal. We are not flexible with that. It is constant. However, we can't control the outcome. We can do everything in our power to convince these two kids that Jesus is real and God loves them personally. We show them scripture, help them understand the Bible, set wise boundaries, and pray with them. We believe and live what we are teaching them. But we have learned that we must be flexible with each season of their lives. Although we can influence them, we really can't persuade them of anything. The choice is up to them; they must decide individually. Moreover, if we are wise parents, we'll use each opportunity unique to each season to teach them to follow Christ.

So we watch for teachable moments. Some we nab, and others we miss. But throughout the course of their lives, we have to bend. They are people, not commodities. They are not robots or clones. Kennedie and Kadison are unique, and they are developing faith in their own ways. God is doing that, so we trust Him to start and finish their faith. Since He is the author, He will write their story—whether or not they live it is up to them.

In the meantime, I help them adjust their lives according to His boundaries. I do that because I know that if they learn flexibility, they will be content and fulfilled. They may not always be happy, but they will be joyful. And there is a difference. I want them to learn to be flexible—not just with others, but even more importantly, with God. If they learn that skill, the sky's the limit, and they will be blessed.

When Kadison was about five years old, he said, "Hey, Mom! Look what I can do! I can twist my body into every letter of the alphabet."

He then proceeded to do just that. Beginning with an *A*, he went through the entire alphabet, twisting and turning his body to shape every letter. I loved every minute of it and laughed out loud on *Q* and *Z*. His creativity astounded me.

Oh, Lord, make me that flexible with You. And please keep me that way. Don't let it be a temporary phase. Help me to be permanently flexible.

When I think of flexible people, I think of those who are pleasant and kind. I don't think of people who fight to get their own way. They're not wimpy, but they aren't rude and self-serving either. While maintaining their values and integrity, they go with the flow. When their plans are interrupted or even changed, they remain calm on the inside as well as on the outside.

Beth Moore Ministered to Me at a Yard Sale

Since one of my personal goals was to get our kids to all forty-eight continental states before their high school graduations, I looked forward to long tours. (We missed it with Kennedie by just four states but still have time with Kadison.)

In preparation for one trip to the East Coast, I cleaned the RV from top to bottom and stocked the fridge. Our youngest niece, Celeste, was coming along, and the kids were super excited. I felt prepared for the upcoming miles and looked forward to the ministry waiting for us.

But then, just hours into the trip, the RV broke down. Smoke was billowing out of somewhere, and we were dead in the water. Sitting in the far lane of a busy country highway, we saw a repair garage across the street. Randy decided to take a chance, so he inched the RV into the parking lot—and sighed. We knew what smoke meant: money. We also knew the small garage probably couldn't fix the big rig and that we would need a truck repair shop.

While Randy talked with the owners, I walked to a yard sale next door. I needed to clear my head, and I didn't want the kids to see me cry from frustration. I picked up a Beth Moore book and randomly flipped open to somewhere in the middle. I read one paragraph. Only one. She challenged her reader to remain calm when calamities come—both big and small. She said that our attitude and reaction to a change in plans proves whether or not we trust God. She continued her point by asking the reader to think of a time when things hadn't gone as planned. (I didn't have to think hard.) "How did you respond?" she asked. I can't remember the book, and I'm not even sure I remember the paragraph accurately. But that's what God spoke to me about. I knew He was telling me to relax and trust Him even though my well-thought-out plans were changing by the minute.

After talking with the mechanic, Randy returned to the RV with good and bad news: they could fix the problem, but it would take days to get the parts. Since there were no other options in the area, we had no choice but to leave the RV right there and rent a car for the remainder of the trip. Within hours, we'd given away all the food I'd prepared and had stuffed our clothes in garbage bags (we had no luggage). The kids snuggled in the backseat of a midsize sedan they thought was "tiny."

I was so frustrated. My clean RV—bedding and all—wasn't going to get us to the East Coast. It was staying there while we moved on. That wasn't the plan, and I was really irritated. I'd worked so hard to make sure we were organized for the upcoming weeks, and it all fell apart.

By the time we got back on the highway, Kennedie, Kadison, and Celeste were singing songs and making up games—loudly. They were excruciatingly loud, all three of them. Their voices monopolized the car, and I soon realized how much space I was used to. I also witnessed their flexibility, which was a great help to me. They were so joyful.

I asked the kids to quiet down so I could say something: "Um, I don't mean to be a Negative Nellie, but where are we gonna stay when we get there?"

We all started laughing, realizing we hadn't thought that far ahead. Crazy as it sounds, we took one thing at a time. Randy called a pastor, explained the situation, and hung up with our answer. One of the churches in Connecticut had an uninhabited but furnished parsonage built by Pilgrims who came over on the Mayflower. The history was fantastic, and we were welcome to stay there.

After a great weekend of ministry, we had a couple of days off before the next round of concerts. We'd planned to go into New York City for the day, but now, since we had the rental car, we decided at the last minute to drive to Rhode Island, Massachusetts, New Hampshire, Maine, and Vermont. Those were new states for us, so we spent a couple of days sightseeing and relaxing on York Beach in Maine.

When we got back to the car, I noticed several missed calls from my Mom. I immediately called her back.

"Everything okay, Mom?" I asked.

"Are *you* okay?" she answered in an urgent tone. "Where are you?"

"Maine."

"Did you feel the earthquake?"

"What earthquake?"

We had no idea there'd been an earthquake and that much of New York City had been evacuated. No wonder she was so concerned!

The earthquake was immediately followed by Hurricane Irene. We waited out the hurricane in the Mayflower house and figured it had weathered a lot of storms before. I kept in close contact with my sister, assuring her that Celeste was fine; she had a bag of Goldfish crackers and a box of fruit snacks to keep her busy. (Celeste likes her food.) We made pallets on the floor in the office area of the house and waited. The storm came right over us, and we lost power.

In the morning, we emerged to see a very mangled town. With trees and downed power lines everywhere, we helped with the cleanup efforts. Picking up sticks, I thanked God that the RV was safe at the garage two states away. Randy quickly reminded us that we could have been in the city when the earthquake hit, and the RV could have been destroyed in the hurricane. But because the RV broke down, we were in a rental car far from the earthquake and safe in a three-hundred-year-old house during the hurricane. God definitely planned the trip according to what was best for us, and He blessed us with visiting the New England states—all while protecting us from harm.

Beth Moore was right.

May It Be to Me

To a flexible person, life is not about getting what he deserves or what is rightfully his but rather about what needs to happen for the greater good. A flexible person does not get rattled easily, and he wants to be stretched. Knowing his boundaries, he stays focused on his mission. A flexible person realizes that God is not required to explain His decisions, but is thankful when He does. That person is a blessing and can be used to a greater capacity because he's willing to follow a plan better than his own.

That's not me—yet. But I am getting closer. Every day, the Lord uses interruptions to make me more flexible—even if the situation isn't from

Him. He still uses it. And He certainly used my time in the passenger seat of the RV for personal growth. It didn't turn me into a doormat; rather, it strengthened and molded me. It became a construction zone for character adjustment.

As young American children, we have been taught that we can do whatever we dream. That's good—it gets us thinking outside the box—but I think a better lesson is that we can do whatever *God* wants us to accomplish through Christ.

For example, Mary, the mother of Jesus—she was young. Some commentators believe her to have been as young as twelve or thirteen years old when she was visited by the angel Gabriel. It was common in Bible times for women to bear children at a young age, but sometimes I wonder whether God chose a young girl because she wasn't "set in her ways" yet. She was flexible and pleased Him with her life. She was the one to carry, birth, breast-feed, clothe, train, clean up after, teach, love, and laugh with His only child, the Savior of the world. And what's wild is that she actually had a choice.

When Gabriel told Mary that she was God's chosen servant, she believed him, even without understanding. Remember: Mary was Jewish, and her family was looking for the coming Messiah. Granted, she probably didn't realize the Savior would come as He did, but nonetheless, she waited for that day just like her ancestors. We can't know for sure, but I doubt Mary thought *she* would be the woman to birth Emmanuel.

Notice that her question—"How can this be, for I am a virgin?" (Luke 1:34)—was in good taste. It wasn't disrespectful or rebellious, but it *was* appropriate. She didn't doubt God's choice; she just asked about the specifics. It took me a while to notice the difference between the two.

What if her response had been like so many of ours when God tries to convince us of His plans? We say things like, "I'm not good enough," "I can't do it," "I'm not worthy of your calling," and so on? Mary, on the other hand, respected God's opinion of her. In fact, His opinion carried more weight than her own assessment of her character, her ability to succeed, and the enormity of the situation. In other words, she trusted Him, even though it seemed impossible. She was abundantly blessed because she believed.

Follow Suit

I'm astounded by Mary's flexibility. Engaged to Joseph when God revealed His plan, it took her in a new and uncertain direction. One moment she was dreaming of her life as Joseph's wife and mother to his children, and the next, she was pregnant by God. In a split second, she was given the opportunity of a lifetime. No, more than that: she was given the singular opportunity in all of history to birth the Son of God. Her head must have been spinning. Life as she knew it was about to change.

Even so, we find her worshipping, pouring her heart out in adoration of God's goodness, justice, mercy, and holiness. She bowed her life before Him and willingly submitted to His plan. She allowed Him to alter her course. I think she *invited* it just by the way she lived. He found her faithful and decided to use her.

Throughout scripture, we see plenty of instances when God used people who were not faithful, but Mary was. He called her to a difficult life, and she had to stand strong against the disbelieving murmurs and careless remarks that changed her social status almost overnight. She could have been stoned to death. But because she was convinced of her Maker and knew to Whom she belonged, Mary accepted God's will and became the only woman to experience the Christ child in her womb.

Even so, Mary was human and needed a Savior just like the rest of us. As her Son hung on the cross and poured out His perfect, sinless blood, He paid the debt of sin—including her own. Mary was ransomed that day just like you and I were. That must have been horrendous for her to watch, and I wonder whether she ever regretted saying yes to God's plan. I highly doubt it. Even though it had to be a tough life, it seems she had a greater perspective.

Flexibility doesn't come naturally—for me, anyway. I've been forced to learn it, or at least, *highly encouraged* to learn it. I have no idea whether it was easy for Mary or not. Still, I want to be flexible like her. I look forward to meeting her in heaven and hearing her perspective on motherhood. I want to thank her for her example of bending with God's plan for her life. I'd like to tell her I tried to follow suit, although my life was far less dramatic.

Ask Big

Though Mary's life was much more difficult than mine, I still need God. While living in the RV, He met me through His Word repeatedly. I discovered new things as the Holy Spirit highlighted passages for me. He used Luke 18:28–30 as a constant source of encouragement:

> Peter said, "We've left our homes to follow you."
> "Yes," Jesus replied, "and I assure you that everyone who has given up house or wife or brothers or parents or children, for the sake of the kingdom of God, will be repaid many times over in this life, and will have eternal life in the world to come."

That promise is for me and for everyone who has sacrificed anything for the cause of Christ. He's paying attention, and He knows the inconvenience. True to His Word, He has repaid our family many times over, which is one reason I wanted to write this book; it's my personal record of His faithfulness. I needed to tell people about the individual attention He gives to those who serve and love Him. I have experienced His blessing in this life and excitedly anticipate abundant blessing in eternity.

Our first Christmas living in the RV was a challenge because I absolutely love Christmas. I crave all the excitement and chaos that comes with celebrating the holidays. Initially, I tried to imagine being crammed in that little space, opening presents without a tree, and no oven—which meant no turkey. I must admit, I was a bit depressed and didn't feel flexible at all.

On the other hand, looking at our calendar, I noticed we had concerts scheduled in California during December. For years I'd wanted to experience my favorite holiday on the West Coast with the sun, waves, and incredible coastline. But mostly, I wanted to celebrate with my sister and her family. Jeff, Keli, Amber, Kierstin, and Celeste lived in California, which made celebrating holidays with them nearly impossible. Yet we were attached to our nieces and missed them terribly. Years earlier (when they lived in Michigan), I'd worked for Jeff and Keli as the girls' nanny.

I'd even been invited into the delivery room for each of their births, and that created an instant bond. To this day, I am grateful that Jeff and Keli gave me the chance to be there which laid the foundation for becoming so close as a family.

Over ten years had passed since we were together for Christmas, but now there was a great opportunity before us. I wanted my mom and dad there as well, which meant flying them from Michigan to California. I also knew there was no way all eleven of us would fit into Jeff and Keli's apartment. There weren't enough beds, and it would just be too tight. I decided that since God was in charge of all of this anyway, I might as well *ask big*. So I started praying.

I wanted to be in a house for Christmas, and since I didn't own one of my own, it would have to be someone else's. It needed to be large enough for eleven of us, and I also needed to use all their stuff: their bedding, kitchen and cooking utensils—everything. However (and this seemed like a potential problem), I didn't want the owners of the house to be *home*. For our family to be alone—just us—sounded like the best Christmas gift.

I sent an e-mail to a couple of friends in California and made one phone call explaining my quandary. I knew I was asking for something out of the ordinary. After all, who in their right mind would invite an entire family to stay in their home the week between Christmas and New Year's?

A few days later, I heard those exciting words "You've got mail" as I double-clicked on my e-mail's inbox. The reply message informed me of the good news: a friend of a friend had offered for us to stay in their beautiful home in Palmdale, California, overlooking the valley. These were people who didn't know us, had never even met us. We were invited for not one but *two* weeks during the holidays while they were on vacation. Not only that, but if Palmdale wasn't convenient for us, another house was available as well! We were given two options. God not only provided a place for us, but He gave us a choice.

Deciding which location and dates worked best for us, I anxiously called the owner of the house to talk about specifics. After I'd introduced myself as "the crazy woman who wants to use everything you have worked so hard for," she said, "We are more than happy to share with you!"

I replied, "I promise we will not steal anything, and we'll leave it better than we found it."

"Oh, honey, my husband works for the government. We aren't worried about you," she laughed.

I reemphasized that there were eleven of us, and five were kids.

"No problem; use whatever you need. Enjoy yourselves!" She even told us to use their food and soda.

Since they were already on vacation by the time we got there, we retrieved the house key from a freezer on the back patio. Everything was exactly as she'd said, only lovelier. The back yard had an inground pool, complete with Jacuzzi and waterfall. The water flowed peacefully under a stone bridge, which became a favorite hangout for the kids and the backdrop of some great family photos. There were beds for all of us and three bathrooms. The traditionally decorated Christmas tree was beautiful, and her kitchen was like a supermarket.

After we unloaded the luggage, including Christmas presents and food, we prayed. In the dining room, we grabbed hands and thanked the Lord for what He had done. We asked Him to bless the owners of the house and draw them to Himself as only He could. We didn't say amen until we promised to respect their possessions and treat everything as if it belonged to us.

After a quick discussion about other people's property and what they were and were not free to use, the kids scattered! They had a blast looking at photos on the walls and trying to figure out who was who. It gave us a better sense of those sharing with us. It helped us picture a family other than ourselves actually living there.

Nothing belonged to me, but it felt like it did. I was amazed. As we were cooking Christmas dinner, I realized I felt right at home. It should have felt foreign to me, but it didn't. It seemed I belonged there, like the place was made just for us. For the first time in a decade, we were able to celebrate the birth of Christ together as a family.

What an experience! I will treasure it forever. That Christmas convinced me that the Lord cares about the details of my life and there is nothing I can't ask for. He planned for us. We simply asked Him where He wanted us to be, and He answered. Through that situation, He built a confidence in me to believe Him even when things seem impossible.

My faith has grown and stretched like a rubber band. As it does, I become more flexible. With each situation, God drives me toward agility.

The road He's chosen for me includes twists and turns and construction zones. He gives and takes away in order to teach me to follow Him. Sometimes it hurts; other times it's fun.

I will say, much like living in the RV, the road of life is lighter without a lot of stuff. The more I give to Him, the more flexible I become. As I unload my junk on Him, He builds my faith through His constant leadership. He doesn't change, but the seasons do, and His consistency reminds me of the white lines on the highway—keeping us within the boundaries of His plan.

The Backseat View

I invite you to swivel your chair and look inward as you contemplate what you just read. Allow the Holy Spirit to shine His light on areas in your life as He instructs, encourages, and builds your faith.

* Like Kennedie in her bunk, discomfort sometimes comes with growth. How have you adapted to changes that have required you to go with the flow?
* In situations of inconvenience, do you find yourself adjusting or complaining?
* It's natural to enjoy consistency in life. Is the Lord taking you through a transition time right now and asking for more flexibility?
* As He did with Mary, is God directing your life in a way that is completely different than you planned? Does it scare or excite you?
* When God answers prayers and blesses you with His supply, do you show your gratitude by immediately stopping to thank Him?
* Have you felt at home in God's presence even while you are far from the familiar?
* Are you lugging a heavy load—adding miles to your journey?

If so, give it to the Lord and enjoy the freedom of a lighter load.

PULL OVER AND ASK
FOR DIRECTIONS

Dollars and Sense

To me, money is a big headache. My bank account balance often limits
what I can and cannot do. Our culture conditions us to believe that our
value is intrinsically connected to how much money we make. We also
have an enemy who threatens us with poverty and lack. (It really annoys
me when he tries to steal what's mine.) Since the love of money is the root
of all kinds of evil (1 Timothy 6:10), I figured God would teach us how
to manage it. I am grateful God doesn't *need* money, but I sure am glad
He has it.

One of the first issues God addressed with us as we were wading
into the waters of full-time concert ministry was not merely money but
the principle of *provision*. We had to learn some tough but crucial lessons
about how God was going to provide for our family and ministry. And
let me say this: We continue to face financial challenges that prove to be a
training tool for developing deeper faith. The longer we serve in ministry,
the more faith we need.

Our first challenge came the first day we were officially self-employed as missionaries to the United States. That Monday we realized we didn't even own a piano keyboard. I know, it seems crazy and irresponsible, but nonetheless, it's true. It was like a window shade was rolled up and we instantly saw the landscape.

The church where Randy worked owned the keyboard we used for occasional worship concerts, and they of course would need it for the new worship leader. We were embarrassed we hadn't realized it sooner. But with no money, it wouldn't have made a bit of difference.

"Tell me we're not going to charge thousands of dollars on a credit card so we can lead worship this weekend for a love offering," I said to Randy, with sweat beads breaking out on my forehead. We weren't two hours into this ministry before needing a life preserver.

"No, we are going to wait for God to supply our need. He has five days," he answered.

So we got on our knees and asked the Lord to provide exactly what we needed—an eighty-eight-key keyboard with weighted keys, by noon on Friday. Peace settled on us, and even though we were watching the clock and looking to borrow or rent a keyboard, we sensed the Lord wanting to prove Himself to us. We thought about shouting our need from the rooftops and calling well-resourced Christians who probably would help us out of pity. But we decided that if God was truly who He claimed to be, He didn't need an advertisement from us. For that situation, we knew we were to stay quiet. So we did. But we kept praying.

On Wednesday of that week, we went to the music store to find the instrument Randy wanted. The salesman tried his best to persuade us to finance the keyboard, and we considered it. But after Randy excused himself, went to the car alone, and prayed, he returned without peace about the purchase. We left the store empty-handed.

We prayed that night, reminding God that according to our calendar, Friday was barreling toward us like a freight train. *Lord, three hundred women are expecting us to lead them in worship this weekend; the hotel doesn't have a piano … what do we do?* Honestly, I wondered how well equipped we were for the road ahead.

Thursday came, and Randy was confident that God was going to supply, so we went back to the music store.

"Why?" I asked, "Nothing has changed."

He said, "I don't know, but I'm sure we're supposed to go back."

We returned to the store and ended up with the same salesman, who was surprised to see us. Again, Randy excused himself, went to the car alone, and prayed.

He came back and said, "I'll take it." The deal was done, and I started sweating.

"How is today different from yesterday?" I whispered through clenched teeth to my husband, who was so sure of his decision.

"I have peace today, and that's all I know."

"Well, could it be because tomorrow is Friday and we're running out of time?" I asked, though not meaning to sound like a doubting Thomas.

We purchased the keyboard with our savings, which had been a parting gift from the church. We'd been saving that money for *emergencies only*, and while some could argue this was an emergency, I didn't want to devour that money so quickly.

At home, Randy unpacked the keyboard just long enough to find a great piano sound and put it back in the brown box. Hoping we had done the right thing, and questioning our decision with every fiber of my being, we went to bed.

We had lost power due to a recent ice storm, and our phone had been out for several days. When we woke up Friday morning, everything was back on.

Just hours before we left for the retreat, a woman called and said she had been trying to reach us but couldn't because the phone lines were down. The Lord had told her to give us a check for two thousand dollars to purchase a keyboard.

"What does that mean?" she finished.

"It's actually twenty-one hundred dollars, and I purchased it last night," Randy replied. He then caught himself and added, "But we can handle the extra hundred. Honestly!"

She insisted on giving the full amount. And when he told her the whole story, she was thrilled to explain why we had had no peace on Wednesday to make our purchase.

"The Lord told me on *Thursday* to give you this money, and that is exactly when He gave you peace to buy the keyboard."

Imagine her joy as she realized that God did indeed speak to her. It built her faith as well as ours.

I recount that situation with specific details because sometimes, when a story is told, it appears to have happened smoothly, without bumps and bruises. Not so. As time passes, we tend to forget the anxiety we had to conquer. There was pacing, there was questioning, and there was doubting. But—more importantly—there was *timing*.

We experienced a myriad of emotions amid the decisions that week. The specifics remind me that God uses details. In the book of Numbers, the Lord gives excruciatingly boring details about territories and the numbers of Israelites in each tribe. It may be fascinating to a history buff, but to me, it's an invitation to *skim*. Regardless of my lack of interest, however, God divulges thousands of seemingly unimportant details.

Yet those specifics are significant whether I realize it or not. We see His faithful hand in details. Imagine God answering a prayer and asking, *Did you notice that I ...?* Remember: God is personal, and His personality can often be seen in the details of His provision. (We have been given two more keyboards since then—both donated by supporters who were sent by God.)

Don't Forget

Whether it's a financial need or some other kind, it's easy to forget what we've asked of Him. Unfortunately, when that happens, we miss the answer. It's *common* to ask and *rare* to remember.

One day, as Randy was attaching the trailer to the RV, his hand got smashed between the trailer hitch and ball; approximately 250 pounds of tongue weight from the 2,500-pound trailer fell on the center of his hand. He turned white and felt an electric shock shoot up his arm.

I grabbed an ice pack and helped him sit down.

"Oh Jesus, oh Jesus, heal him," I said, trying to catch my breath. It flashed through my mind that life, as we knew it, was about to change.

How could he play the piano? I suggested that we head to the ER, but we decided to give the Lord time to answer our prayer for healing.

During the concert the next morning, as Randy was ripping off one of his lively boogie pieces, I realized I had forgotten all about his hand. I don't know how, but I did. Suddenly the Holy Spirit said, "Ya know, I healed his hand last night."

I cried. God had answered our prayer with a miracle, but somehow we'd overlooked it. As soon as Randy finished playing, I told the people what had happened. And with tears rolling down his cheeks, Randy backed up my testimony: "I can't believe we forgot. It was major, and God healed me so completely and instantly that I missed it."

The congregation applauded and cheered for God. Randy and I made a pact to notice what God does, and to keep watch for His miracles.

> Be still in the presence of the Lord and wait patiently for Him to act. (Psalm 37:7a)

An Aha Moment

I had to learn that God is the answer to our every need—emotional, physical, spiritual, relational, and financial. His provision covers it all. He continued to prove Himself to us and still does. There is no end to the trials, tests, and challenges, though they do change from season to season. When I learn about His character, a deep work happens, and I trust Him more.

Just as a child runs to his parents for everything from a popsicle on a hot summer day to advice about a college major, we run to God for everything. We run to Him *in* everything and *with* everything. He doesn't have to answer like He did with the keyboard or Randy's smashed hand, and many times He doesn't. But He does provide. And generously too.

Learning about God's provision has affected every area of our lives, but mostly our peace. At times when we didn't have strength to serve Him,

He made us strong. When we were anxious, He calmed us. When we were sick, He healed us. When we didn't know where our next paycheck was coming from, He supplied. And one of the most important lessons was learning to trust Him with our finances. We found that since our heart follows our treasure (Matthew 6:21), it was really important to give Him what already belongs to Him. So we tithed on every dollar He provided. It wasn't legalism; it was obedience.

When I started to worry, I would pray, "Lord, we have not robbed You. Malachi chapter 3 says that we should bring the first of what we make to You. If so, you will open the windows of heaven and pour blessing on us. We have done that, and we need some of that blessing right now so I can send the mortgage payment."

One time Kennedie and Kadison received Easter cards from my folks, with ten dollars tucked inside (money instead of chocolate bunnies). The kids were thrilled; you would have thought it was a million bucks. After a few minutes, I took Kadison's ten-dollar bill and tucked it safely in my wallet. He was compliant, knowing I would save it for him. Kennedie, however, put up a fight.

"No, Mommy, I want to keep it."

I told her, "You might lose it, so let me take it. It still belongs to you."

She continued to resist: "I'll put it in my pocket. It's mine!"

The situation escalated as I tried to have an adult conversation with a six-year-old. That's when I said, "Give me your money, and when you need it, I'll give it to you."

Before I'd closed my mouth, the Lord spoke loudly in my ear: "Ah-ha! Did you hear that, Marli? 'Give me your money, and when you need it, I'll give it to you.'"

My heart leapt with joy because I heard Him. What He told me changed my perspective about His provision and trusting Him as my source. It also made me think about the God of all creation *talking to me*. I saw Him as a caring Father, committed to taking care of all that I have, all that I need, and all that I am.

No Safety Net

A couple years before we bought the RV, we traveled in an SUV that pulled a trailer with our sound system. Leaving our house for months at a time, it was a challenge to make enough money for all of our travel expenses and personal bills while funding the ministry as well. It was tight, and we had no surplus. We don't really have any now either, but back then it was a new level of trust for us. Today, we are used to waiting on God; we've experienced His provision so many times that we're confident He will continue to supply. Today, it's familiar territory, but years ago, it was like forging a path to the Wild West—knocking down trees, cutting through mountains, and encountering unknown terrain that made us tremble even before pulling out of the driveway.

I imagine that's how the disciples felt when Jesus told them to go and preach the gospel to distant cities—without a walking stick to lean on, a suitcase with a change of clothes, or money for travel expenses:

> Don't take any money in your money belts – no gold, silver, or even copper coins. Don't carry a traveler's bag with a change of clothes and sandals or even a walking stick. Don't hesitate to accept hospitality, because those who work deserve to be fed. (Matthew 10:9–10)

He gave His disciples a mission and sent them without the necessary supplies to sustain themselves from day to day. I wonder if they questioned Him verbally or whispered behind His back, discussing the obvious dilemma it made for them as travelers. What did their parents think? (There were a lot of things we didn't tell our folks, just because we didn't want to worry them.) Many of the disciples were young and left jobs to follow this rabbi who claimed to be the Messiah, the Son of God.

As he did for the disciples, the Lord took us on a journey without the means to get across the country or even to the next state. But we went because we were certain of our mission, were convinced of our calling, and trusted His character. We had to learn the countercultural lesson that money is never our source of power.

So traveling in the SUV, we went to Florida for two months and helped a small church develop a worship team. They gave us a weekly paycheck, which, although generous considering the size of the congregation, was only half the amount needed to make our weekly budget. We still owned a house in Michigan and needed housing in Florida for those two months as well. We found a small rental house for January and February, and two separate parties paid the rent for us. Again, unsolicited and right on time. That in and of itself was miraculous.

Our plan was to schedule concerts on Wednesday and Sunday evenings and use the CD sales and love offerings to offset the shortage. However, we quickly realized that we were not wanted in the state of Florida. Other than three concerts, Randy was unable to book our open evenings. Doors were continually shut. Things got so desperate that Randy told pastors we would volunteer our time, in hopes of selling a few CDs. The response was "No thanks, we're fine." The rejection was so obvious that we didn't return to the Sunshine State until several years later. (Fortunately, Florida now welcomes our ministry, and we visit there regularly.)

Hindsight reveals that the Lord designated that season as training. At the time, we were discouraged and scared; we couldn't pay our bills, couldn't schedule concerts, and were spiraling further and further into debt. I tried my best to trust beyond what I could see, but sometimes my emotions got the best of me. As the bookkeeper of our ministry and household, I kept track of the numbers, and everything looked bleak.

A few weeks into the tour, Randy said, "Honey, the Lord has been speaking to me, and I think He wants us to give away half of our salary."

"What? Give half our salary away? Do we have to tithe on it first?" I couldn't believe it, and honestly, I thought I couldn't be stretched any further. How wrong I was.

"Randy, I know the numbers, and we have a stack of bills. You realize we're going down, right?"

All he said was "I know. Wanna go down giving?"

Hmmm. That was an interesting idea, and silently I revisited Malachi chapter 3. God said to *test* Him with our giving. In fact, it's the only place in scripture where God gives that challenge. I wondered if He actually meant it—and then chastised myself for wondering. Thinking for a minute, I decided, *Of course He meant it; my life isn't a game to Him.*

"Okay, let's do it. We tithe first, cut everything in half, and give the rest to whomever God tells us to."

I'm not sure what we expected, but we had an instant peace and even a giddy urge to give every dollar that came in. (I don't recommend doing this unless you really believe God is asking you to.)

At the end of two months, we were almost thirty days late on our mortgage payment, but we were still giving. It seemed irresponsible and futile. It wasn't. It was obedience. It was a test—no, it was an *exam*.

Pulling out of the church parking lot after our final concert in Florida, I opened the manila envelope that held the love offering. I knew it was going to be gigantic. It was going to be the mother lode of all offerings, and the Lord was going to use it to fix our money problems in one fell swoop.

It wasn't, and it didn't. The offering was ninety-eight dollars. No mother lode, no gigantic check, no quick fix to our money problems.

What were we thinking, giving half our salary away? I asked myself, and instantly relinquished everything I knew to be true. I turned on God and my husband. I looked at Randy and said, "Well, here we are, experiencing the first time God has failed. In all of history—He chose to let *us* down. I cannot believe we are in this situation after obeying Him. What's He doing?"

Unlike me, Randy is a steady soul, rarely rocked by circumstances. I, however, got the drama gene and can be laughing one minute but crying the next. "Reel it in babe, reel it in," he often says to remind me of my passion that often leads to roller-coaster emotions.

Miracles Still Happen

After counting the combination of crumpled tens, fives, and single dollar bills, I said, "We are hundreds short of what we need. Hundreds."

I explained that I had saved a little money from some CD sales and told him of the measly amount in our bank account. When added to that day's love offering, we were still hundreds short. I remember thinking, *I shouldn't be surprised, because I knew how much came in and how much went out.*

Now, I'm no math whiz, but it wasn't that hard to figure out—especially because the numbers didn't have that many zeros. If more goes out than comes in, you'll have a shortage. We started the tour short, so why was I surprised we were still behind?

"Count it again," said Randy.

I did and got the same amount. We were hundreds short. It was quiet in the SUV as we drove. Randy looked at me with peace and strength.

"Count it again."

I did, and to my amazement, when I added it up the third time, it was all there! We had enough to pay the outstanding bills. It wasn't enough to go shopping or make a life-changing investment, but it was enough to write a check for our mortgage payment.

I can't explain what happened in the car that day, because I really don't know. Maybe God hid the extra money from my eyes on the first two counts, or maybe He physically multiplied the money in my hand. I have no idea. But I do know that what happened was miraculous. I counted it correctly the first two times, but only the third time was it enough. No one will ever convince me otherwise. Since I kept track of the numbers, I knew the totals.

God did the impossible with our finances and provided for us in a way I could not foresee. In those moments, I picture Jesus—eyes fixed on me, arms folded, grinning ear to ear, elbowing the angel next to Him, saying, "Watch this. Watch what I'm going to do for Randy and Marli."

I'll never forget feeling His faithfulness: relief, thankfulness, and indescribable glee. It was downright *fun*. But I also felt regret. I had been so quick to judge the Lord as a failure, and I lacked the patience and stability it took to keep trusting Him.

Even with a small offering, God was faithful. He doesn't fail. He *can't*, regardless of my perception. With limited perspective, we evaluate God's decisions, and usually what we deem to be a failure, He proves a success.

With compassion and mercy, He continues to develop godly characteristics in me that I need to walk in faith. He uses situations like that one to stretch me, and even though it's hard, it's always for my benefit.

I apologized to the Lord for having such a strong opinion about how *He* should answer *my* prayer. Even now, years later, when we're in a bind, we name that miracle and then—we rest.

I think that's one reason Jesus sent the disciples without money. He grew them in confidence and trust so they would serve Him faithfully even when all seemed hopeless. The tests and trials God ordains for each of us are not random. He designed them with a very specific purpose in mind. Our response reveals the depth of our trust in Him.

Am I willing to follow beyond what seems reasonable? Do I think there's a limit to what I should be asked to do? Does God want me to look like a fool? Maybe, just maybe.

Due West

As I read what I've written, I notice a pattern: God led us day by day. It was almost as if we were blind to the next day. Good thing, too, because I don't think I could have handled knowing what was to come.

The end of those two months in Florida found us reeling from God's miraculous provision. We'd been flying high for about fifteen minutes when we realized we had to drive from Florida to Southern California for our next set of concerts. Since the Florida church had run out of money and were unable to pay us for our last week of service, we had no money for travel expenses. We had plenty of work scheduled in California but no way to get there.

Just like the Israelites, we were cranky, weak, and fickle. We decided to go home. We told the Lord, "Unless You show up, we're throwing in the towel, hitting I-75 North, and crawling home with our tails between our legs."

Not even two hours later, the pastor from Pasadena who'd hired us to teach a marriage seminar called with God's answer: "We decided we are not paying you enough to come all the way to California. We are adding an extra three hundred dollars. It'll be waiting for you when you get here."

What? Who does this?! We've been in ministry a long time, and, I assure you, that's extremely rare (but very much appreciated). Budgets are tight, tithing is down, and the economy is fragile. We never want to hurt a church budget, which is why we prefer love offerings. But that day, the pastor was God's voice saying, *I am calling you on a journey without an extra cloak or bag of money. Wanna go?*

Since we didn't have that money in hand, the question still gnawed at me: *How are we going to get to California with* no *money?* Nonetheless, we knew where God wanted us to go and decided that if He could part the Red Sea, He could get us to California.

We spent the last night in Florida, with friends from the church. This couple was dear to us, and we laughed a lot. Since the husband was leaving for work early the next morning, we hugged him and said our goodbyes before going to bed. We slept well, even though we didn't know what the morning would bring.

After a great breakfast, we packed the car. The kids were tucked safely in the backseat, but I was shaking. I couldn't believe we were about to get on the expressway and start the twenty-five-hundred-mile trek across the country with hardly any money. I thought we were not only crazy but irresponsible. I kept looking at the kids, thinking, *I am so sorry, I promise to pay for your therapy when you're older.*

As Randy started the engine, we were already hot because the Floridian sun was doing its thing. We were fastening our seat belts when we heard a car horn beeping frantically from behind us. Looking in the rearview mirror, we saw our friend, who had already left for work, running up to Randy's car window. He handed him a stack of cash.

Out of breath as he was, he managed to explain: "I was in my office, and the Lord said, 'Hurry! Go to the ATM and get five hundred dollars for Randy and Marli.'" Then he added, "That's so crazy. I've never heard the Lord speak like that before."

He was excited, and we were relieved. I doubt they realized how God used them to spur us on to deeper faith. They literally paid our way to the West Coast. Their obedience made all the difference on our journey. Because they yielded to the Spirit, we were able to go. They sent us. It was a much bigger deal than just getting us to California for a marriage conference, because that test molded our faith. I think that's another reason Jesus sent the disciples without money. It gave others an opportunity to support ministry and provide for God's servants. It stretched more that just the disciples.

One person's obedience, in the hands of God, can change the world.

Chicken Teriyaki

We were careful with the gift. Even with that amount of money, it was hard to eat well. So we ate at gas stations. Two hotdogs for a dollar could feed all of us for five bucks, including drinks and nachos. But as you know, even the biggest junk food eater gets sick of a constant diet like that. Kadison was four years old at the time and still in a car seat. His little voice came from the backseat: "Daddy, do you need gas yet? I'm hungry."

"What in the world am I feeding my family?" I asked Randy, as we drove through New Mexico. With all of that time on our hands (and sick of the alphabet game), I posed a question to get everybody laughing: "If you could eat anything right now, what would it be?" I was just kidding, and it didn't really work anyway. The kids started shouting, "Pizza, pizza!" I think I heard popcorn and ice cream as well. But I wanted healthy food—fresh vegetables and protein. Something substantial to eat, something you feel like your body will thank you for. My vote went for a Japanese steakhouse. The tables are fashioned around a large, steaming hot hibachi grill, and the chef comes to you. It was dinner and a show. I thought it would be fun to take our sword-loving son someplace where he could watch his chicken being flipped, diced, and grilled right in front of his eyes—not to mention the onion that is turned into an erupting volcano.

We started salivating over the thought of ginger dressing adorning a cold, crisp, fresh lettuce salad, and an appetizer of grilled shrimp. Mmm ... I couldn't think of a single reason *not* to go there for dinner, other than, of course, the money. It wasn't even an option. It was just a silly game we were playing to pass the time on a long highway with two kids who needed to be entertained.

Approaching the outskirts of Albuquerque, Randy kept the joke going and said, "I'll tell you what: we have to stop at the next exit for gas. If there's a Japanese steakhouse, we'll go."

Minutes later, we ramped off the highway. The only billboard at the end of the exit ramp said, THE JAPANESE STEAKHOUSE. Randy and I burst out laughing. Then he got quiet.

"Oh no, honey, it was just a joke. You are not considering this—I mean, you didn't really mean it." I rambled on as he bit his lower lip and scrunched his forehead as he does with deep contemplation. I knew the look well, and it concerned me. My husband is a thinker. He thinks—a lot. Less than a hundred yards from the billboard, he pulled into the parking lot of the restaurant and turned off the engine. He needed a minute to think, so we just sat there. Kadison had no idea what was going on, but he was quiet anyway.

Asking me what I thought, I told him exactly what he already knew: "It is irresponsible to spend our money like this. God didn't give us that money to go to an expensive restaurant. Besides, it would use most of our remaining gas money, and then what would we do?" He nodded in agreement. Then I added, "*But* you are the head of our home, and if you say we go, I'm in!" I want to say I was joking, but I would be lying.

He finally said, "I know it was just a joke, but God was in the car when I said it. He heard it, and He wants us to go. Everybody out."

I was thrilled and scared to death at the same time. I was hungry too. (Not hungry like *people starving in Africa* hungry, just like *I've been eating too much junk food* hungry.) As we walked to the entry doors, Randy and I felt a flood of peace.

The Japanese steakhouse was just opening for the day, and employees were scurrying around finishing up last-minute chores for the early-dinner crowd. The seating hostess escorted us to a table with a family of six seated at the other end. The cooking style of a Japanese steakhouse makes for a unique seating arrangement, and unless you have a large party, you end up sitting with strangers. The idea is to fill up each table so the chef is cooking everyone's meal at the same time.

The family we were seated with had four children, all younger than ours. Instantly, I was irritated. I silently said to the Lord, *Father, in the past two months we've driven from Michigan to Florida and then Florida to New Mexico with two kids in the back of an SUV, all without a TV! The last thing I want right now is to sit with four more kids.*

I could tell Randy was thinking the same thing as he let out a little groan. We smiled politely and greeted the couple as we gave our drink orders. Then the show began. The chef was extremely skilled with sharp knives, yummy fresh veggies, rice, and butter—oh, the butter! He sprinkled soy sauce over everything and tossed an egg and caught it on the flat edge of his knife with ease. It was apparent he had done this a time or two.

Kennedie and Kadison loved every minute of it, at least until Kadison saw the flames; cautious child that he was, he didn't like fire being set to sizzling oil. But he loved the onion volcano.

The fresh food was fantastic, and we ate our fill and then some. I tried to focus on the fact that I was caring for my family by feeding them something other than hotdogs and nachos. I kept my mind busy instead of wondering how we were going to make it the rest of the way to California.

We finished our meal, thankful that all six children were very well behaved. Everything went well, and we didn't even have time to enter into conversation with the family at the opposite end of the table. They were busy with their kids, and we were busy with ours.

"We're ready for our bill," I said to the waitress.

She replied in a very thick Japanese accent, "It's taken care of."

Obviously, we had a language barrier problem, so I slowed my speaking pace down and spoke louder like I usually do when speaking to a foreigner: "Oh, I mean, our bill. The check, so we can pay." Then I reminded myself that she wasn't deaf, just Japanese.

She looked irritated and matched my volume, "It's taken care of—they pay for you." She carelessly waved her hand toward the other end of the table. The young couple was busy, wiping four little mouths and collecting their belongings.

We sat, stunned, and finally said, "You paid for our meal?"

They smiled and nodded as if it was no big deal. For me, the restaurant fell silent, and I no longer needed to breathe. In the spirit realm, God pushed the Pause button and let me take in the moment.

God Kissed Me

I quickly thanked them and rambled as I told them our story. "We're missionaries to the United States, and we traveled from Michigan to Florida and a billboard sign and hot dogs and half our salary and a rental house and love offerings …" I was in such shock that I mumbled incoherent details, not even in the right order. Little of what I said made sense. My recollection was sketchy at best. Assuming this young couple had heard straight from God, directing them to buy our meal, I recounted the recent events that had brought us to a Japanese steakhouse in Albuquerque, New Mexico.

The woman simply looked at me and said, "Pardon me, what's a missionary?"

In that moment, the Lord taught me a priceless lesson. He can provide for me *anytime, anywhere*, and through *anyone* He chooses. We gave them a couple of CDs, thanked and hugged them, and got into the car.

With tears, I said, "I feel like God reached down and kissed me on the forehead." We sensed God telling us, *I can provide for My children whenever and through whomever I want—even people that don't know Me.*

We basked in the blessing of that experience for miles, and I never tire of telling that story. It still sends chills up my spine. Granted, one meal is not the Grand Canyon of life; but the lesson God taught us actually is.

It was good for me to follow God, especially when I couldn't foresee His provision. He proved Himself faithful. That day, He drove us to a restaurant and bought our dinner. I just rode along and looked out the window.

The Backseat View

I've told you some pretty amazing situations when God showed Himself to us in unique ways. Hopefully, you know I only tell these stories to bring attention to God's faithfulness. The only way I know to do that is to tell you what He has done in our lives.

Over the years, people have asked me why they haven't experienced similar situations. I can't be sure. But I too can hear other people's testimonies and ask, *Why hasn't God done that in my life?* In any case, I have found those questions to be futile. What I have found to be helpful is asking God to move more obviously in my life. Oftentimes I pray, *Lord, help me see what You're already doing for me. Help me to notice Your heart and Your hand. I want to see You, but it's tough sometimes. Open my eyes, Lord.*

I also think that because we followed God, He was able to teach us according to *His* lesson plans. Like a good teacher, He decides what to teach us and when. The *how* is up to Him as well. It's important to remember that the lesson is the goal—not the story behind it.

To follow God and trust Him in the journey has been the most exciting adventure we have encountered to this day. He has a never-ending feast of blessing planned for us, and I don't want to miss a single meal.

Swivel your chair and think for a moment. Ask the Holy Spirit to remind you of a time when He showed Himself to you in a very real way. Then answer these questions:

* What was He trying to teach you?
* How did that lesson change your perspective?
* Do you know how to wait for Him to act, or do you take matters into your own hands?
* Have you ever read Malachi chapter 3? Do you believe it?
* What does tithing say to God about your trust in Him as the source of your money?

Please know that if you are not currently a tither or do not understand that scriptural principle, you should not feel condemnation. I share our story with you so that you may experience the same blessing we have. If you want more information on tithing and giving, let me suggest an awesome resource: *The Blessed Life* by Pastor Robert Morris of Gateway Church in Southlake, Texas. You can buy the book or watch the series online at *www.gatewaypeople.com.*

Kennedie and Kadison traveling in the back of the SUV.
("See no evil—speak no evil—breathe no air.")

My kids, all grown up.

Kennedie, after twelve years of homeschooling, graduated and participated in a homeschool ceremony where she sang one of her original songs.

Kadison and me in Connecticut just before Hurricane Irene.

The kids and me at the steps of the Supreme Court in Washington, DC, where we led worship for the National Day of Prayer for Hurricane Katrina.

Randy, Kennedie, and Kadison at the St. Louis Arch.

All four of us on a ferry, going to sing at Mackinac Island Bible Church.

Arriving on beautiful Mackinac Island. (L to R: Dear friend, Blythe Bieber; my mom (seated), Shirley; family friend, Patsy Clairmont; and me.)

The four of us at Ground Zero, New York City, with an open phone as our friend Ernest sang his song in memory of the fallen towers.

A quick snapshot of me in front of our poster displayed in a store window.

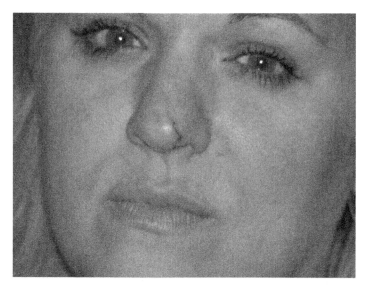

The war wounds of ministry: a dog bit me on the nose
ten minutes before a concert. Had to sing anyway.

Me in the recording studio.

Me at a Laundromat with about twenty loads of laundry.

Me trying to get cell phone reception in the hills of Kentucky.

Randy and I ministering together at a Sunday morning concert. He has always been such an encourager for me to share my testimony.

Randy and me singing at the Java House coffee shop in South Lyon, Michigan.

My perspective from the platform. What an honor
to worship with so many wonderful people!

Randy and me during a sound check. You just gotta have fun.

My handsome husband and look-alike son
during the setup for a concert.

The four of us during a Sunday morning concert. This
is the third keyboard provided by supporters.

Randy and me in
Boston on a day off.

My favorite picture of
my best friend and me.
(Photo by Heather Iafrate)

Our newest family member: Macy Lucille, the teddy bear dog.

My three traveling buddies and me, just moments after buying a house after eight years of living in the RV. Kadison is holding the house keys.

YIELD

I'm a Murderer

I killed my dog today. Well, actually, I hired a hit man—I mean, a hit *woman*. I paid Dr. Amy forty dollars to inject him with a solution to stop his heart. The blood money included disposing of his body so I wouldn't have to. Nor did I have to pay immediately; she billed me. I didn't even pay with cash—I wrote a check.

I wept bitterly. Actually, I sobbed. I gasped for breath in the vet's office as I said *good-bye* and *I love you* and finally, *Thank you for being such a faithful friend.* I bent over Sammy as my tears soaked the fur on his chest and he struggled to stay with me. We looked into each other's eyes, knowing we only had a few minutes left together. I knew it, and he knew it; I don't know how, he just did. He knew he was leaving.

I loved that dog, took care of that dog, and depended on that dog. We spent twelve years loving each other as master and servant, and as companions. He was always excited to see me, always willing to snuggle, and he listened like none other. Plus, he rarely had an opinion that differed from mine. We were inseparable.

He belonged to us for twelve of his fourteen years of life. Fourteen years isn't a long time for a human, but it is for a dog. I am ashamed to tell you that I loved that dog more than I love a lot of people. He was easier to love and easier to get along with. His only opinion was about soybeans and cauliflower, which I don't care about anyway. He loved both of those things, crazy as it was. I couldn't get him to eat the most expensive dog treat, but put edamame in front of him, and he was thrilled.

Sammy traveled with us in the RV for most of the eight years that it was our home. Sometimes we would leave him with my parents, but most of the time we had him with us. It made the RV feel more like home when he was curled up on the couch while we bounced down the road. I could be homesick, miserable with a cold, broken down on the side of the road, or parked in a Walmart parking lot, but it helped to have Sammy there. He was the friend that never said he had to call me back or didn't feel like talking. Sammy was a playmate for the kids, not to mention the best high fiver on the planet (especially when beef jerky was involved).

People all over the country grew to love Sammy as we visited year after year. Rarely rambunctious, he represented the bichon frise breed well and was an excellent lapdog. Bichons were bred to sit on the laps of royalty, or so I read somewhere. He was lovable, and everyone said what a sweet dog he was.

Sammy was never an issue because he stayed in the RV, other than when a pastor invited him into the church building for a change of scenery. He loved racing through the halls, darting in and out of open doors.

One time we ended up staying with a church secretary and her family for a week because an ice storm froze the fresh water tank (which crippled the RV). To our horror, Sammy lifted his leg on her laptop, which was sitting on the living room floor. Other than that, we had no problems with him.

When we'd leave Sammy in the RV to go into a grocery store or movie theater, he'd stand on Randy's seat with his front paws on the steering wheel. Eyes fixed on us, his triangular head would follow us until we were out of sight. We called it an isosceles head. When we returned, the first thing we'd see was his little noggin watching for us. Usually all the lights, fans, and wiper blades would be on because he'd stepped on all the switches located on the driver seat armrest.

As the four of us were walking into a grocery store one time, we heard the faint beeping of the RV horn. Sure enough, it was Sammy. We heard a long, constant blare of the horn as if he were saying, *I think you forgot to take me with you!* We laughed and sent one of the kids back to stay with him while we shopped. We figured if he was that desperate to be with us, we couldn't leave him alone.

But today, we said goodbye. Sammy never licked any of us, but he used his last breath to kiss my cheek in a final show of affection and subservience. He mustered enough strength to stretch out his tongue and wipe away my tears as I said *goodbye.*

I hate goodbyes. I hate pain, sickness, and death. I hate separation. I hate all of it.

And we should. We weren't created for separation. We weren't created to say goodbye. That was never part of God's original plan for us. We were meant to stay in relationships for eternity. We were created to experience faithfulness, loyalty, affection, friendship, and trust. Why? Because those are attributes of God. As we are filled with His Spirit, we should demonstrate those attributes with one another. But most of the time, my dog was a better example of those things than I am. Of course, he didn't talk—that had to help.

By now, the non-dog-lovers reading this are losing their place on the page because they keep rolling their eyes. That is, if you even make it this far into the chapter. But give me a chance to bring this home. Remember: this is my story of how God convinced me to let Him transform me from the inside out. And trust me, He used my dog.

See, when my dog died, I spent months agonizing over his death. I didn't grieve that much when I lost my grandparents. I didn't cry that hard when the twin towers fell. And I didn't ache like that when I learned that nearly sixty million babies have been legally aborted in America since 1973.

I didn't grieve as much because those deaths don't affect my everyday life. I can go on just fine. I can live in my little corner of the world because I am not the one starving or imprisoned for my faith or martyred for the sake of Christ. I don't even grieve that much when I slander someone's name or silently stand by and listen to gossip. Somehow, I can justify that. Can you relate?

But now, my dog is gone and I have to cry. And God understands because He made us for relationships, even with pets. But when I get to the heart of the matter, God wants me to grieve the latter things more. People are much more important than pets. We are made in God's image; animals are not.

Don't get me wrong—animals are definitely God's creation. And they are important; God made a covenant with them as well as humans in Genesis chapter 9. Furthermore, Romans 8:20–22 teaches us,

> Against its will, all creation was subjected to God's curse. But with eager hope, the creation looks forward to the day when it will join God's children in glorious freedom from death and decay. For we know that all creation has been groaning as in the pains of childbirth right up to the present time.

All of creation, even dogs, groan for restoration. But they were not made like God, to reflect His glory. We were. And since we were made for a relationship with Him, it should result in resembling Him. We were created to experience love, joy, and goodness as we relate to one another. That was His plan, but obviously we got sidetracked somewhere along the way.

God revealed my heart when Sammy died. He uncovered a heart that was callous toward others—a heart that should ache with someone else's loss. A heart that should break over a lost soul. He showed me a heart that should be molded by the Potter's hands but that in some ways has decayed and metastasized into a lump of dense stone. Why am I like this?

Could it be because hurting people are everywhere and I doubt I can make a difference? Maybe it's because I am too consumed with myself to reach out and love someone. Am I quiet during gossip because I know I have been guilty of the same thing, and I don't want to be labeled hypocritical? Am I just comfortable in complacency? What if I am simply tired of trying to convince those who don't believe?

When Sammy died, I realized I needed a heart transplant. I needed a fresh sensitivity to others, and I needed to learn how to act more like my dog. Faithful, constant, loyal, trustworthy, and I desperately needed more naps. Naps are the definitely the ticket.

Then I snapped out of it and realized that God doesn't want me to be more like my *dog*; He wants me to be more like *Him*. He is the faithful, loyal, steadfast friend I have always needed, and He talks—but He doesn't gossip. Aren't you glad God doesn't gossip? Let's talk about gossip. Wanna? No? Me neither. Let's put it off just a little while longer.

Let's Change the Topic

I'm reminded of a worship seminar Randy taught when he defined the Greek word for worship (proskuneo). According to Strong's Exhaustive Concordance, *proskuneo* (or *proskyneo*) means, "to kiss, like a dog licking his master's hand". Randy explained it like this: a dog enters a room, identifies his master, and sits close enough to kiss his hand. He explained that worship has just as much to do with proximity as it does position. I thought about that for a long time. A dog feels secure in his master's presence, resting at his feet; I think Sammy felt that with me. He also was fulfilled. At least, I think he was, because he never actually said that, but he did show it.

Proskuneo is a beautiful picture of God and His children. God wants us to relax in His presence, showing Him affection as we sit in close friendship at His feet. I've heard people label God as egotistical, wanting all the praise for Himself. To that I say, He's the only One who actually deserves praise, and He never mishandles it. You and I do, but He doesn't.

Proskuneo implies that we bring nothing of inherent value to the Master but simply desire to be in His presence. To enjoy, be content, and rest by the Master's side.

But, I am of value, you are of value, and we bring ourselves—so what does it mean?

Mulling this over, I see the value in just *being*. Not *doing* but *being*. See, that's what I liked about my dog. He did nothing for me. He just was. How could I love someone so much who did absolutely nothing over the course of twenty-four hours? He had a crook in the end of his tail, very few teeth, and mounds of warts. *Best of Show* was not in his cards. I don't have that much grace for my husband or my kids, and certainly not for myself. But

129

God does. He gives me grace and an open invitation to just be with Him and experience a relationship that will never end.

Then that *being* with Him produces a motivation to serve Him. Suddenly, my being with Him becomes a catalyst for change. Instead of constantly *doing*—a worn-out worker trying to turn the tide of culture—I become a friend of God, slowly becoming more like Him.

I will never cry in a final moment with Him. He won't say goodbye and leave me. We'll be together forever. God is my constant companion, loyal confidant, and trustworthy friend.

And He wants me to follow suit with you: To be more gracious. More merciful. More compassionate. More aware. More loving. More there. More faithful and more committed to what He cares about—people. After all, people and the Word of God will last forever. Those two things will never end. I have decided to invest my life in both of those.

Separation Anxiety

It was common knowledge that Sammy had a serious separation anxiety problem. He was restless and unsettled if we weren't together. He had to be with us. What if you and I were like that with God? Maybe you are, but at times I've wandered from Him and somehow gotten through the day anyway.

What if our joy and contentment depended on sitting at His feet? What if our very lives depended on the meaning of the word *proskuneo*? I think they do. I think we're miserable when disconnected from Him, but we're so used to it, it becomes normal.

I also think the separation anxiety we feel when not intimately connected to Him is dulled by the enemy's roar, which sounds confusingly similar to life. It seems that we believers have gotten really good at *doing* and not so great at *being*. Such busyness affects the way we love others. It affects the way we respond, forgive, and reconcile with each other. It affects everything about each one of us.

Satan likes that because he knows it's in the *being* that we will experience true friendship with God. He also knows it is in His presence where we find the very thing we were created for: relationship. Satan knows that when we truly experience a relationship with our Maker, we will be whole. How exactly does he know this? Because he once had it.

What if we allowed the feeling of separation anxiety from God to change the way we live? Change the way we love? And finally, change the way we talk about each other? What if I refuse to gossip because I've been with Jesus and He thinks so highly of you that I can only repeat the good He says about you?

I Told You It Would Reappear

Proverbs 6:16–19 says,

> There are six things the Lord hates, seven that are detestable to Him: haughty eyes, a lying tongue, hands that shed innocent blood, a heart that devises wicked schemes, feet that are quick to rush into evil, a false witness who pours out lies, and a person who stirs up conflict in the community.

So when I talk about you with evil intent—to slander your name—I am just as bad as someone who sheds innocent blood? That's what He said. At the very least, He listed them together and detests them both. Every time I gossip or slander, I attack your character and value and murder you with words. And when I witness against you falsely, I take your life in my hands. That's how powerful words are.

> I am surrounded by fierce lions who greedily devour human prey — whose teeth pierce like spears and arrows, and whose tongues cut like swords. (Psalm 57:4)

When we gossip, lie, or talk about each other with anything other than good intent, we act as murderers. No hit man needed.

I remember when my middle niece, Kierstin, was three years old. Her older sister, Amber, was in kindergarten and responsible for the class gerbils over Easter break. (Well, maybe they were guinea pigs, but it doesn't really matter.) Their names were Barnum and Bailey, and they were ugly little rodents with stray bits of wiry hair.

Since I was the girls' nanny, I was at their house over the holiday. Kierstin loved holding the gerbils, and I was concerned she might drop one, but not enough to tell her not to carry them around. After all, they weren't puppies; they were gerbils or guinea pigs. Whatever. I was downstairs in the kitchen when I heard a bloodcurdling scream from the upstairs bath.

I ran up the flight of stairs to find Kierstin screaming, "I'm a murderer! I'm a murderer! I killed him!"

There on the tiled bathroom floor lay Barnum—or Bailey; I'm not sure, because I never could tell them apart. I didn't care, anyway. But he was dead. Well, not dead, just unconscious. The poor thing was motionless on the cold floor, and Kierstin, still screaming, was inconsolable. Chaos ensued as Keli and Randy ran to see what the nanny couldn't handle.

Randy scooped up the rodent and rubbed his back, just like they did with the runt in *101 Dalmatians*. Sure enough, he began to breathe. Over the next twenty minutes, that little guy fought for his life and won. He slowly started to use his front feet to push himself up and drag his body across the floor.

It was pathetic and very intense as we cheered for the rodent struggling to walk again. Finally he was on all fours, steadily making his way around the room. Kierstin was trying to catch her breath from the horror as I attempted to convince her that she could not, indeed, be labeled as a murderer.

But we can. We bring death with our words. We suck the life out of people by what we say and use language to inflict wounds that take years to heal. Words are dangerous because as soon as something is said, it can never be *unsaid*. You can apologize, but it's impossible to reverse. Words destroy relationships. What we say has the potential to rob us of the very thing we were created for: relationships.

What if we responded like Kierstin? What if I considered my words so weighty that gossip to me was a crime? Like breaking the law—inflicting so much pain that the course of history is forever altered.

Not only so, but what if we believed the opposite to be true as well? If I can murder with words, then I can bring life with words.

> The tongue has the power of life and death and those who love it will eat its fruit. (Proverbs 18:21)

What Is Gossip?

I wanted to give you an example of when I gossiped, but I can't think of one. So instead, I'll tell you about a time my sister gossiped, and it was horrible. You will not believe what she did. Keli opened her big mouth and really messed things up—in fact, embarrassed the whole family.

Well, that was ironic.

I merely want to shed light on a difficult but common issue that divides churches, friends, and families. We saw it in the body of Christ all over the country. Gossip crosses denominational lines, socioeconomic classes and geographic regions. It spreads like wildfire and is just as deadly. That's why I am addressing this issue. So let's get really specific because I think it's the only way to move past this issue and grow in Christ. We have to define it and name it and avoid it—purposefully.

According to one definition, *gossip* means "to spread rumors or secrets, speak about someone maliciously behind their back or repeat something about someone else that you have no right to repeat." (See Leviticus 19:16; Proverbs 11:13; 16:28; 20:19; 25:23; 26:20–22; Jeremiah 6:28; 9:4; Psalm 41:7; Romans 1:28–32; 2 Corinthians 12:20; 1 Timothy 3:9–11; 5:13–14; 2 Timothy 3:1–5; and Titus 2:2–3.)

I've done this, and you probably have too. It can be subtle, but sometimes it's obvious and we stop midsentence. Other times, we blaze right past the check in our spirit and finish the conversation; it feels too good to stop talking.

Here's the point: gossip is sin, and it destroys relationships. And here's the scary point: where there's gossip, rarely is there *only* gossip. In 2 Corinthians 12:20–21, Paul is speaking to the believers in Corinth about his next visit when he says,

> For I am afraid that when I come I won't like what I find, and you won't like my response. I am afraid that I will find quarreling, jealousy, anger, selfishness, slander, gossip, arrogance, and disorderly behavior. Yes, I am afraid that when I come again, God will humble me in your presence. And I will be grieved because many of you have not given up your old sins. You have not repented of your impurity, sexual immorality, and eagerness for lustful pleasure.

Through Paul, the Holy Spirit is telling us that gossip is a breeding ground for other sin. Gossip produces hostility, anger, jealousy, pride, and behavior that does everything but glorify Christ.

Did You Hear?

Why then is it so easy to talk about other people?

There are a couple of things I have learned about the "whys" of gossip. First of all, most of us are insecure in some way, and talking critically about someone else makes us feel better. We learned that in first grade, and it's still true. If I put someone down, where am I putting them down *to*?

Below myself.

When I gossip, I elevate myself above you, which is ungodly. Philippians 2:3 says to think of others as better than ourselves. In other words, I should put you above me.

The second reason I think gossip is easy is that I can be spineless (but I label it as graciousness). I don't want to hurt your feelings by speaking up and coming across as self-righteous. And I don't. I don't want to be or even *appear* self-righteous.

Sometimes when standing for truth, it seems like we are judging. Yet consider this: a judge renders a sentence, and his word is final. The culture of today says that if Christians have an opinion about anything—we are judging. What's worse is that the Church has believed that lie, and even promoted it.

Of course, standing for truth, defending the gospel, and restoring someone in sin should only be done in gentleness, love, and authentic graciousness. But we've got to learn that when all is said and done, *it must be done*. I think some Christians have confronted sin with such a mean spirit and for so long that nobody wants to do it anymore. It's easier to just cave and let sin run its course. But that won't benefit any of us.

Lastly, gossip is hard to stop because it usually happens among friends, and it's hard to confront friends. It's embarrassing and awkward and can be relationship changing. But consider Matthew 12:36–37:

> And I tell you this, you must give an account on judgment day for every idle word you speak. The words you say will either acquit you or condemn you.

That's Jesus talking. I quiver when I read that verse, and I should. How embarrassing will it be to give God a reason for every idle word I've spoken? Maybe it shouldn't be so hard, after all, to nip gossip in the bud. Relationships are vital, but not more important than honoring God.

Is It Gossip or Not?

Regarding gossip, sometimes I get confused. Maybe you'll relate, or maybe you've matured past this. I, however, have gotten stuck with two things: warning others of false teachers and discussing a problem (with an outside party) when restoration is the goal.

As for the first issue, in Acts 5:1–11, Luke told the followers of Christ to beware of people like Ananias and Sapphira, who lied about the amount of money they gave to the disciples for God's work. Luke named them; he called them out. Granted, they were already dead because of their sin, but he used them as examples of what not to do. It seems like gossip, but it wasn't. It was a warning.

Before Ananias and Sapphira died, Peter, with a grieving heart, confronted the couple urging them to repent. He mourned the sin committed against the Holy Spirit, because it was self-serving. They didn't repent, and it cost them their lives. That is sobering. Whenever we get calloused to sin, we should read this account. It sharpens our senses to the seriousness of sin. My sin, your sin, and our nation's sin.

Secondly, there comes a time when we should warn others about a false teacher or liar. In that case, we'd better make sure we have our facts right. We also need to make certain that we do so with a heart for restoration instead of revenge and judgment. If I am excited about calling you out, my heart is not in the right place, and I probably shouldn't be the one to do it.

Remember: even if something is true, it can still be gossip, and repeating it can "stir up dissension among brothers" (Proverbs 6:19).

Let Go of My Tongue

We've had the honor of building relationships with pastors and their wives all over the country. One aspect of our ministry is partnering with servants wounded in battle. The pastor and wife of any congregation can be attacked, but they also can be the attackers. In most situations, I can't tell the difference because I wasn't there as an eyewitness of the conflict. But we have spent many hours listening to pastors and church leaders talk about dissension in their flocks over seemingly inconsequential issues.

Randy and I have prayed for God's help to keep our hearts pure. We want to help resolve conflicts that affect countless congregations.

Moreover, God has put us in a unique position; we are safe because we leave *and* because we have a broad perspective on church ministry. Have we helped? I'd like to think so, but sometimes I'm not so sure.

All in all, I have been extremely impressed with pastors and their carefulness to discuss a difficult situation without gossiping. Don't get me wrong, I have heard a lot of gossip—sometimes I joined in and other times I simply didn't stop it. So I don't say what follows lightly; I thought long and hard about it to make sure it is true. But I do believe that in all our years of ministry, I've talked with more pastors who genuinely want help than ones who just want to throw somebody under the bus.

If you've had a different experience, I am very sorry. It's terribly unfortunate to witness one child of God slandering another. But just remember: we're all human and make selfish choices from time to time. Pastors should dissolve gossip, not fuel it. Sometimes they do, and sometimes they don't; sometimes the leaders need more transformation than the followers.

When I was in sixth grade, I went to a really bad doctor. Maybe he was at the end of an awful day or maybe he was just mean; I don't know. He wrapped gauze around my tongue, held me down, and shoved tweezers down my throat to remove a fish bone. He could have—and should have—been much more gentle and kind. But he wasn't. It scared me to death, but I still go to doctors.

Don't leave the local church because someone mishandled you. Find a healthy body of believers and plant yourself there. Become part of the solution to resolve conflict biblically. Don't be the kind of person who shouts loudly about the importance of grace, but in reality, extends very little of it to others. Those people are a dime a dozen and rarely do they live healthy spiritual lives.

I have learned there is a proper time and place to discuss difficult issues. I also am convinced that it must include steps toward a resolution, which acts like a balm for a festering wound. The book of Proverbs talks about gossip *and* wise counsel. We have plenty of biblical instruction on both, so we know there is great value in conversations that include steps for restoration and healing.

Does that mean the person I talk to has to be directly involved in the situation? Not necessarily.

More Guacamole, Please

We went to lunch at a Mexican restaurant with a pastor and his wife one day. I love these two, a lot. While munching on nachos and salsa, the pastor asked us how we were doing—really doing. Living on the road, traveling constantly, raising kids, and being married—he wanted to know it all. So since he asked, we unloaded on him.

We spoke from the deep recesses of our hearts. At the time, we were in the middle of a conflict (outside our family) that we couldn't change. We had no decision-making power to fix it, and believe me, if we had, we'd have resolved the whole thing peacefully and quickly.

But we couldn't, and we were miserable. Well, I was miserable. It seems that men move past conflict quicker than women. Randy and I were in the same book but on different pages. He healed quicker, forgot faster, and extended a longer arm of grace than I.

After describing the situation in detail, and through tears, I tried to convince them of how many hours I'd spent praying about it. I won't ever forget what this pastor said:

"Marli, I am going to tell you something that most pastors would never say to you."

Suddenly, it didn't matter how good my taco salad and pinto beans were; he had my undivided attention.

He continued, "Stop praying about it."

I said, "Excuse me? Did I hear you correctly?"

"Yes. You have taken it to the Lord so many times that this issue has become an obsession, and it's time to move past it even without a resolution."

Instantly, I was set free.

Later that night, I had one final conversation with the Lord about the matter: *Father, we have talked about this issue so many times there is nothing left for me to say, except that I want to be clean before you and honoring to you. I am leaving this in your lap. You do with it what you want, and if I need to do anything, just let me know. I'll do whatever you say.*

I was a different girl. There was a lightness that filled me like I had just lost twenty pounds. I was able to let it go. That's the day I learned that wise counsel is very different than gossip. I received solid instruction, and (to the credit of the pastor and his wife), a possible gossip session turned into a day of deliverance.

Tell Me What to Say

Because it's hard to think on your feet, most of us have probably walked away from conversations wishing we'd handled them differently. I've found it helps to have a sentence or two in my head for on-the-spot responses. It may be uncomfortable to use them, so let's not put each other in situations where we'll need to. But just in case, here are a few ideas, along with some other practical steps to combat gossip:

* Politely change the subject. They'll get the message. Adding a positive comment can defuse the situation as well. A positive word can always be spoken.
* Say, "Hey, let's pray about that right now." Then pray, and afterward add, "Hopefully that helps you with the situation." Then change the subject.
* Say nothing. Stay silent, and when they are finished speaking, simply say, "I am not sure what you want me to do with that information." I know it's bold, but you also can say, "If you don't want me to do anything with that information, I would rather not be responsible for it."
* Before you begin a conversation (by text, e-mail, phone, or in person) decide what is appropriate to talk about and what is not. We all know our hot buttons, and we need to be aware of what to avoid.
* If you still find yourself gossiping—ask someone to hold you accountable.

What Does This Have to Do with My Dog?

I started this chapter by telling you I killed my dog. We put him to sleep because he was in tremendous pain and dying. We loved him and with the help of a veterinarian made a really tough decision. Obviously, it was an act of mercy.

But with gossip, there is no act of mercy and slander is never loving. As disciples of Jesus, we should grieve gossip.

This is a hot topic because most of us know churches that have closed due to splits and divisions, often involving gossip. There may initially have been a legitimate problem, but gossip was like gasoline thrown on the fire. Relationships have been destroyed because conflict wasn't handled well, and slander, malice, and jealousy became the preheated oven for gossip.

But God designed us to live as a family. We *are* a family; we are God's children, which makes us brothers and sisters, and we all know how miserable siblings can be (except mine, of course). It's time to make a concerted effort to resolve our issues with wise counsel among ourselves. We ought to be mature enough to do so, though history has proven we are not.

On the rare occasion that our beloved Sammy held a grudge against me, I found it took a lot of effort to win him back. If he was really mad, he refused to look at me, and he sighed a lot. He threw a canine temper tantrum. So I bribed him with cheese and rubbed his belly.

Because he was a dog, he couldn't talk, but he did communicate. He made it abundantly clear that he wanted nothing to do with me. His body language told me that I'd been gone too long and should have been more considerate of his needs. He couldn't say it—but he did tell me. I'd work hard to restore our relationship, and finally, he would come around and forgive me.

Sometimes I left him too long, and sometimes he peed on my carpet. So in the end, we both had things to forgive—if we wanted a relationship.

The Backseat View

Kennedie doesn't like the beginning of this chapter. She doesn't think my description of Sammy's death illustrates my point, and at first she wanted me to eliminate it. I considered it, but in the end didn't. Maybe I will change my mind, but as of today, I think it reveals my heart accurately.

We had to come to an agreement because her relationship with me is much more important than any illustration or story I could tell. Both Kennedie and Kadison read this book and okayed every story that included them before I turned it in. (Okay, let's be honest; I couldn't get Kadison to actually read the book, so I just read every part *about* him *to* him.) I had to do it that way out of respect for them. See, this is their story too. I am telling it, but they lived many parts of it with me, and it belongs to them as well.

Sometimes we don't agree. We don't always see eye to eye, and negotiations have to be made. But I couldn't stand publishing a book without their consent, because I have been their mother a whole lot longer than I have been an author. (And one day, they could be choosing my nursing home.) Anyway, after a heartfelt discussion, Kennedie reconsidered, and this chapter remains unchanged.

There are, however, a few stories I will treasure in my heart alone—as a mom who loves her kids and respects them greatly—even though you'd get a good chuckle out of them. But if I didn't consider their feelings, what kind of relationship would we have? I imagine one with bitterness and dissension.

I don't know about you, but I refuse to live with unresolved issues in my relationships. Tension is miserable and it erodes intimacy. Of course, I can only keep peace on my end; the other party is responsible for themselves. Long ago, I made the personal decision to keep short accounts with God and people, apologize and own up to my sin. Not one of us will go through this life without the need for a true relationship with God the Father. How we grieve sin, respond to hurts, forgive each other and admit our own failures will determine the intimacy we have with Jesus and each another. Without doing any of those things, it is nearly impossible to sit close enough to kiss the Master's hand.

It is time to swivel your chair and think of an occasion you wish someone had considered your feelings. Now, answer these questions:

* How did that situation change your relationship?
* Was gossip involved?
* What could you have done differently to resolve the conflict?
* Is there anything you can do today to bring resolution?

Now think of a time you should have been more sensitive to someone else and ask yourself these questions:

* How did I cause dissension?
* What can I do to mend the relationship?

Ponder this:

* How much time do you spend *being* instead of *doing*?
* Are you sitting at your Master's feet, enjoying His company?

And finally, ask the Holy Spirit to show you how you can be an asset to the family of God.

* How can you bring unity and minimize division?
* Are you holding any grudges?

With God's help, we *can* get along.

> So encourage each other and build each other up,
> just as you are already doing.
> (1 Thessalonians 5:11)

BRIDGE MAY BE ICY

Scaredy Cat

Oh Lord, I have come to You for protection; don't let me be disgraced. Save me, for You do what is right. Turn Your ear to listen to me; rescue me quickly. Be my rock of protection, a fortress where I will be safe. You are my rock and my fortress. For the honor of Your name, lead me out of this danger. Pull me from the trap my enemies set for me, for I find protection in You alone. I entrust my spirit into Your hand. Rescue me, Lord, for You are a faithful God. (Psalm 31:1–5)

I trust in that passage. I could fill the rest of this book with passages like it that have been a shelter to me. I've shared my bout with fear and anxiety publicly only a handful of times, only when I sensed the timing was right. And honestly, I'm not sure I totally understand it yet myself. It takes a good, long while to deal with personal struggles that feel normal, dysfunctional as they may be.

I do, however, know exactly when the black cloud of anxiety made its home right over my head: the moment our daughter was born. It sounds terrible, but it's true. I was focused on myself and didn't realize at the time just how much it had to do with having a new baby.

Most of the time, I was worried about me—except for a repeated nightmare I had for what seemed like years. I would wake up panicked not knowing what to do if I were on a huge boat in the middle of the ocean and dropped Kennedie overboard. I repeatedly woke up in anxiety attacks, desperately trying to devise a plan of action.

Randy would look at me and say, "Honey, when was the last time we were on a boat? And if we were on a boat, why would you hold our daughter over the railing?"

Even in my waking hours, I constantly tried to reason a way out of situations I wasn't in. It was miserable (and still is, if I allow myself to return to that dungeon).

My primary fear was that I would contract some awful life-threatening disease and would not live to raise this beautiful child. I worried a tragic accident—like a plane falling out of the sky—would take my life and leave her alone. Now I know it was the fear of death, but it took me years to figure that out.

It had little to do with my confidence in caring for her and the daily responsibilities of being a new mother. I wasn't worried about that a bit. In fact, after four years of nannying my nieces, I knew a lot about caring for infants. I wasn't concerned about Kennedie, really; I was worried about *me*. If I had a nickel for every thought I had about me, I would be a wealthy woman. The details about those seven years are better left for another time, but you need to know the basic facts so you understand what a challenge it was for me to walk away from health insurance.

At that time, I depended on Blue Cross/ Blue Shield to protect me. If I had a pain, I ran to the doctor. If I saw a commercial on TV advertising some particular health test, I thought I needed it.

Even though Randy didn't understand panic attacks and night terrors, he stayed by my side and prayed for me endlessly. I would soak in the bathtub and sob. I cried so much during those days, I kept Kleenex in business from my sales alone! Randy wanted to fix everything, but there was no tangible problem to solve. There was nothing to fix—well, except me.

Eventually, I went to a Christian counselor who was extremely helpful. I pictured the therapist saying, "Wow, you really are messed up. I just don't know what to do with you."

Instead, she said, "Well, I can see why you feel like that."

Rarely has a sentence brought such balm to my soul.

I have a deep compassion for anyone going through depression, fear, and especially anxiety. Waiting for the hammer to fall is an awful way to live, and the constant conversation in my head was loud and chaotic.

I used that season of life to search the scriptures like never before, and many nights I fell asleep with my head resting on my open Bible for comfort. It was as close as I could get to God; I just held on and waited for the storm to pass.

God used those seven years of difficulty to strengthen me, and eventually I followed Him across the country, even without health insurance. That took believing He would be with me even in sickness and danger.

We found ourselves at a crossroads when we discovered we could no longer afford health insurance. When we left the church and started the concert ministry, we were suddenly responsible for our own benefits. Even the cheapest insurance was impossible for our budget. We had a choice: pursue a career that would provide insurance or stay faithful to our calling, following His plan and wait for Him to work it out. The choice was obvious, but we wondered what would happen if one of us suddenly got sick.

As we prayed, I realized that if something happened, God would either heal us or provide the money for medical care. I know it sounds simple—it is. I also know there is somebody reading this saying, "Marli, you have no idea how expensive sickness is." You're right, and actually, I didn't need to know. I needed to know what God wanted us to do. He was the driver, and we were the passengers, so in essence, we decided to ride. We moved ahead without insurance (and went without it for twelve years). Some thought we were nuts, but many of our friends were in the same boat as we were. That helped me, and in retrospect, this act of faith was a giant step in my deliverance from anxiety.

If I Die, I Die

Queen Esther decided to go uninvited to see the king and plead for the lives of the Jewish people. Because it was legal for the king to kill anyone who came into his presence uninvited, she risked being put to death. So Esther called for a fast and asked for God's favor. Resolving that issue, she said, "If I die, I die" (Esther 4:16).

I can hardly compare my life with hers; however, her response helped me. I decided to do the same thing and adopted her attitude. Now, whenever fear knocks on my door, I answer it saying, *If I die, I die*. It sounds morbid, but on the contrary, it's quite freeing. Once I realized that God is not only the keeper of my life but also of my death, I was able to start living again.

Because Jesus conquered death, I get to rise again. His victory is my victory. Esther showed me the importance of maintaining an eternal perspective while seeking Him who literally keeps my heart beating.

During those years of anxiety, I imagined some pretty crazy illnesses, accidents, and tragedies. But I never imagined what happened to us late one night while driving through Alabama.

Daddy, Can I Help?

We were driving the SUV and pulling the trailer, and we stopped at an out-of-the-way gas station to fill up. It was late, and Kadison was asleep in his car seat while I was relaxed in the front passenger seat. Randy and Kennedie fiddled with the gas nozzle. She wanted to help, so Randy let her squeeze the nozzle while he stood right beside her.

While squeezing the handle with all her might, she accidentally pulled the nozzle out of the tank just a bit, spraying gas all over her. It looked like she had been dunked in a ten-foot pool of gas. She was dripping in the foul-smelling petroleum. Both she and Randy screamed, which caused me to bound from the car. I tried to piece together what had happened as I looked at her beet-red face.

"My eyes!" she screamed. "Mommy, my eyes burn!"

I was holding a bottle of water in my hand and instinctively dumped it all over her face. She was getting redder by the second, and her skin was starting to swell.

A couple from two pumps over saw the whole thing and shouted, "We're calling 911!" Immediately I said, "No, wait. Not yet."

Looking back, it was the Lord speaking through me, because with my fears, the first thing I would have done was call an ambulance. Instead, they waited, and we rushed her into the gas station.

We were in the bathroom with her head in the sink, trying to splash water in her eyes. It wasn't working very well because of the angle of the sink, and she was sobbing—but I was calm. Even today, I am surprised at how calm I was. My heart broke to watch her suffer though, and in the back of my mind I was thinking about her precious eyesight. *Oh Jesus, protect her vision.* But even in the middle of that, I experienced this peace I am unable to explain.

The gas station attendant bolted through the door and led me out of the ladies' room to a brand-new, tiled shower. They had a beautiful, private shower, which had been completed only days earlier. They had brand-new towels, soap, and shampoo for us. None of it had ever been used. We were the first.

So within three minutes of gasoline spraying into her eyes, Kennedie was showering in one of the loveliest ceramic-tiled showers we have ever seen. I'm not exaggerating when I say that the Hilton has nothing on this little gas station.

I never understood why that gas station would install a shower. It wasn't on a main highway with a lot of truckers; we've been to plenty of those. This gas station was in the middle of nowhere. I can't help but think that God put that shower in just for Kennedie.

She stood in the shower for quite a long time and let the clean water pour over her face and wash away the gasoline. The attendant told me to use as much water as we wanted and gave us as long as we needed. She was kind and handed me an unopened Bausch & Lomb eye rinse she just happened to have in her purse.

Kennedie put on clean pajamas but was a little embarrassed to come out of the shower room. I explained the customers were waiting to see if we needed any help and that they just wanted to make sure she was all right. Sure enough, the couple that offered to call 911 was still there, waiting.

"I have never seen someone act so calm and cool in such a scary situation," the lady said to me.

I told her, "You just saw the grace of God in action." But on the inside, I was thinking, *You have no idea.*

Not until we bought Kennedie a much-deserved Slurpee (Kadison got one too, just because) and were pulling back onto the freeway did I realize that I'd never imagined such a scenario. The Lord said to me, *Marli, it's impossible for you to think through every crisis that might happen. Just know that I will be with you no matter what.*

Then I lost it—tears, and lots of them. But this time I cried tears of comfort and gratitude.

Reverent Fear

After thirty years of reading the Bible, I am still amazed at what God allowed people to experience, both good and bad. Both ends of the spectrum are mindboggling to me. He asked Abraham to kill his long-awaited son, but He let John view heaven.

The Bible is filled with people who have been through every imaginable situation, and most unimaginable ones as well. Only God could think of a worldwide flood, dancing in a fiery furnace, or surviving a lion's den. I can't imagine giving birth at ninety years old or feeling a tongue of fire rest on my shoulder. I have a good imagination, but I could never dream up those scenarios.

Sometimes when I think about the people who actually went through this stuff, I get depressed. My empathetic heart takes over, and I start to question God's motives. That's always dangerous ground. Actually, it's more like quicksand.

Nothing will swallow me alive faster than believing that God is anything but good. No matter what happens, who it happens to, or even how it happens, God is *good*. He only makes right choices, and His heart is always for us—no matter what life looks like.

Sometimes I wonder if we value life too much. Do you think that's possible? Take the ninety-year-old man on life support whose family is praying for a miracle. I mean, when is enough, enough? Maybe I will feel differently when it's my dad at the end of his life.

Years ago, I heard the testimony of a young boy who was on his deathbed. His parents pleaded with God to heal him and even refused to accept anything but a miracle. That boy was healed and then grew up to be a murderer. When giving their testimony, the parents admitted that although the miracle was a gift, had they accepted his death instead of bargaining with God, life would have been much different for a lot of people.

What if the death of that child would have actually been an act of mercy? After all, God is love. His very nature is love because of who He is.

However, that love may look odd to us because we are conditional creatures that rate everything by its effect on us personally. We judge God's actions as wrong and think He needs our opinion to make an informed decision.

But He did just fine before any of us were created. He *created* life, and He knows exactly when it should begin and how it should end.

> I am the Lord, and there is no other; apart from Me there is no God. I will strengthen you, though you have not acknowledged Me, so that from the rising of the sun to the place of its setting people may know there is none besides Me. I am the Lord, and there is no other; I form the light and create darkness, I bring prosperity and create disaster; I, the Lord, do all these things. (Isaiah 45:5–7 NIV)

For years I read this passage and tried to accept what God said. Sometimes He causes disaster. Many Christians don't believe or accept this. And I can't lie—it's been difficult. But when I really think about it,

I can't help but worship Him because of His power. Some people think that's fear; it's not. Believe me, I know fear, and there is a difference.

My worship is a reverent agreement that He is Almighty God who can do *what* He wants, *when* He wants, *however* He wants. For years I've heard people say, "I won't serve a god who causes disaster. If He's so loving, He wouldn't let that happen." I thought about that statement for a long time and searched the scriptures, knowing He would teach me about His character. What I learned was a necessary backdrop for traveling the country. It might seem overly dramatic, but if I was going to enjoy eight years in an RV traveling to new places, I needed to trust Him to the very core of my being. I had to reconcile myself to the fact that sometimes bad things happen but that He will help me through them. It's simple and life changing—if I believe. As our driver, God mapped a route for us that wasn't always comfortable or safe.

Surrounded

We drove through Baton Rouge, Louisiana, in the month of March one year. I remember because it was the middle of March Madness (the NCAA college basketball playoffs), and Wake Forest had just walloped Texas in the first round.

It was late afternoon when we pulled into Walmart and chose a spot at the back of the parking lot near an IHOP restaurant. It was marked specifically for RVs, and we were the only one there.

Most Walmart stores allow RVs to park in their lot overnight, free of charge. It's smart business because they know there's a good chance we'll come into the store for a gallon of milk and end up buying fifty bucks' worth of other stuff. While living in the RV, we probably spent hundreds of nights in Walmart parking lots across the country.

That day seemed like any other, but we were in for the scare of a lifetime. We were tired and ready to stop for the day, but it was early, so we took the kids to an ice cream parlor within walking distance of Walmart.

It had a red-and-white-striped awning and white wrought-iron chairs with red seats. We pulled two of the small tables together and grabbed an extra chair for our oldest niece, Amber, who was traveling with us. Kennedie and Kadison loved having their older cousin along, as it was a change from their daily routine (not that there was anything routine about their days).

After a creamy dish of ice cream, we walked back to Walmart to stock up on supplies. Returning to the RV after shopping, and pushing our cart through the maze of cars, I recalculated the receipt in my head and wondered how *bare necessities* could add up to a hundred bucks. I heard Kennedie mumble something about driving a couple more hours before we hunkered down, but both Randy and I said we were ready to pop in a movie and just relax. She pleaded with us to continue driving:

"No, I think we should keep going," she said, trying to get my attention.

"Honey, why don't you want to stay here? There's an IHOP; maybe we'll go there for breakfast," Randy told her, using pancakes to try to change her mind. It didn't work.

"Dad, please listen to me. I don't feel safe here, and I really want to go."

"Ken, we walked to the ice cream parlor. You felt safe there, and Walmart seemed fine. What doesn't feel safe?"

"I don't know." Then she continued, with reasoning far beyond her 13 years of life, "Mom, you know how sometimes you just have this gut feeling, but you can't explain it? That's how I feel. I'm not sure why, but I think we should go."

We didn't. We should have gone, but we stayed. We told Kennedie to trust us and relax. We tried to calm her nervousness and get her mind moving in another direction as we climbed aboard the bus and unloaded the bags from Walmart: "Here, babe, help me unpack the groceries. Think about something else," I said, as I rearranged the refrigerator items to fit the milk and coffee creamer.

After watching a movie, we bedded down. That night, Kennedie slept on the couch, and Amber took her turn sleeping on a pallet on the galley floor (which couldn't have been comfortable).

About three o'clock, we were suddenly awakened by an incredibly loud crashing. It sounded like a garbage truck was slamming a dumpster up and down right outside our bedroom window. We were in such a deep sleep, it seemed as if we were moving in slow motion. It was chaotic, and we couldn't grasp what was happening.

Randy and I both stirred and looked at each other in utter confusion. He parted the mini blinds to look outside. Right there, within inches of our RV, was what I call a thug mobile. It had all its doors and trunk opened, with the base speaker blaring its music aimed right at our bedroom window. The sound of the drum beat and the rapper screaming something we couldn't understand (which we were thankful for) was so deafening that we had to shout to hear each other.

"What's going on?" I screamed, as loud as my groggy voice would let me. I wiped sleep from my eyes and tried to untangle my nightgown from around my knees.

Peeking through the blinds, we gazed in disbelief. What we saw was mind blowing. There were hundreds of college-aged youth and gangs of kids doing anything and everything. We saw fighting, drugs, partying, drinking, sex, and people running and chasing one another. It was complete chaos, and we were surrounded. Hemmed in on every side, we were in the middle of a free-for-all.

I looked toward the galley, worried about the kids. Amber was staring directly at us with eyes opened wide as saucers. She too was in shock. Surprisingly, Kennedie and Kadison were still asleep; I quickly asked the Lord to keep them in deep slumber.

We jumped out of bed, trying to gather our thoughts. As Randy hastily grabbed the first pair of jeans and sweatshirt he could find, he screamed at me to call 911. I squeezed by him in the hallway to get to the galley where my phone was sitting on the counter. Hands shaking, I dialed 911 and motioned for Amber to stay away from the windows.

Randy passed through to get to the front. Just then the 911 operator answered, but I could barely hear her, even with my other ear plugged with my finger. I yelled into the phone as loud and clearly as I could, reminding myself to stay calm so she could understand me: "We are in the Walmart parking lot in an RV, and we are surrounded by gangs of kids. Please help us!"

Her next question did nothing to calm me: "Have gun shots been fired yet?"

"Not yet!" I said, realizing we were in true danger. I scolded myself for not listening to Kennedie the night before.

The situation had already been reported, and she assured me the police were on the way.

"Hurry, please!" I said, in one final attempt to convince her of our situation. She did her job well but was so calm that I wondered if she believed me. I guess I wanted somebody else to panic too.

Hanging up the phone, I grabbed Amber and pulled her close with my mouth to her ear. We stood in the kitchen between the refrigerator and stove and hugged tightly. I prayed out loud so Amber could hear, and then I realized I was shouting. With the mayhem outside, I doubted she could understand me anyway. I asked God to deliver us and reminded Him that He is our protection and shield.

"Help us, Jesus!" I said, as I noticed tears in the eyes of my oldest niece who had come with us to experience a memorable journey. *Well, you wanted an adventure*, I thought to myself as I pulled on a pair of sweats.

Amber asked if we should move the kids to the floor, which was a good idea; but they were still sleeping, and I knew God had answered my prayer to keep it that way. So we decided to trust Him with both kids, but especially Kennedie, who was sleeping right under the largest window in the RV. I was thankful that Kadison was in his carpeted cat box, which seemed safer.

Randy sat in the driver seat with the front windshield curtains still closed from the night before. The room-darkening curtains blocked out all sunlight and street lamps and kept outsiders from peering in, assuring privacy. He started the RV engine and sat there for a minute.

"Why aren't we going?" I asked him, with an urgency to put it in drive.

He reminded me that we had to give it a few minutes to warm up so it wouldn't stall as we were driving away. The diesel was dependable, but it needed time to get the oil moving through the engine block.

I felt a pit in my stomach when I realized we had to open the curtains. Until then, no one knew whether people were in the RV or not, and fortunately, no one had tried to break in. We couldn't tell whether anyone tried to pry open the trailer hitched to the back of the RV. A lot of people ask us if we are hauling motorcycles, and I knew that could be tempting.

"Okay, open the curtains," Randy said as he grabbed the panel on his side. I pulled the passenger-side panel to the driving position, which opened up the whole windshield. As soon as we slid the curtains back, we saw the enormity of the situation. There were people everywhere, and the chaos was indescribable. IHOP was packed with people standing shoulder to shoulder. The waitresses held their trays with plates of food high above their heads just to get through.

Amber said, "Those poor waitresses. I feel so bad for them right now." We both agreed.

Then we saw policemen chasing people in every direction, yelling orders with weapons drawn.

Just as Randy put the RV into reverse, a car darted from the rear and blocked us in. I wasn't looking at the back-up camera, so I didn't understand why Randy wasn't going.

"Go! What are you waiting for? Get us out of here!" I shouted above the madness.

"Just another minute," he said, praying the car would move so he could back up just enough to clear the cement barrier he had parked a little too close to the night before. He promised himself that in the future he would park in a place where he could pull straight out rather than needing to use reverse.

But now, we were pinned in. At that moment, we were sitting ducks with a huge windshield everybody could see into. Before the car behind us moved, a girl dressed only in a shirt jumped out and began fighting with the driver. Randy looked away but saw enough to realize they weren't there to pin us in. They had their own issues.

"Don't go out there Randy, please don't go out there!" I probably shouted it more than twice. He reassured me that he wouldn't unlock the door. All of a sudden, the couple got back in the car and sped off. Immediately, Randy backed up enough for the front tires to clear the cement barrier, put us in drive, and eased through the crowd.

There we were, forty-five feet long, slowly escaping through gangs who had their own agendas. Just then, more police cars sped into the parking lot, and people scattered. We looked no one in the eye, pulled out of the parking lot, and ramped onto the nearest highway.

Just as we pulled out of the lot, Kennedie woke up and looked out the window.

"What's going on?" she said, not knowing how right she'd been just a few hours ago.

Randy explained that it was March Madness, and we'd been smack dab in the route of the people traveling home from the big game the night before. We'd picked the wrong place, the wrong night, and the wrong IHOP. It was an explosive atmosphere.

And it seemed like no one had seen us. It was like we were in a bubble and floated right through the craziness. One guy glanced at me, but I prayed he would ignore us, and he did, just like everyone else. Nobody seemed to notice that we were in the spot they'd chosen to party the night away.

Safely on the highway, Amber looked at us and said, "So does this happen to you often?"

We burst out laughing. It was the comic relief we needed. Then we drove about an hour to another Walmart parking lot and asked Kennedie if she felt safe. (Kadison never did wake up.) Since both Amber and Kennedie were wide awake, we decided it would be best if I slept with Amber in the front and Randy slept with Kennedie in the back. We tried to calm them down enough to sleep by talking about heaven. We talked about the great banquet and tried to imagine what kinds of food will be there. We talked about the river, and streets of gold, and people. But most of all, we talked about the safety we'll feel—to never think about pain, danger, or sickness—and how amazing that will be.

Just then a car pulled alongside us, with music blaring almost as loud as the car back in Baton Rouge. I jumped to my feet, wondering if we had been followed, and looked out the living room blinds. It was sheer coincidence; a customer was just sitting in his car checking his receipt, completely unaware of us. He soon pulled away. Unbelievable.

Finally, we slept.

Rest Areas—Test Areas

I wondered why God hadn't chosen a different route for us; why go through Baton Rouge on that night? But then I realized—He did. He used Kennedie to tell us to keep going, but we didn't listen.

Even so, He stayed with us in that nightmare. Compared to what others have endured, that night was nothing. But He taught me about His presence in the midst of danger, and it proved to be a valuable lesson. From time to time, I revisit that night and thank the Lord for His protection.

> For He will order His angels to protect you wherever you
> go. They will hold you up with their hands so you won't
> even hurt your foot on a stone. (Psalm 91:11–12)

That wasn't the only time He protected us.

We were somewhere in Missouri, and it was time for dinner. Randy had to pull off for a break and watched for the nearest rest area. I looked in our *Exit Book* (it told us of every rest area, with its amenities) and found nothing for at least twenty miles.

Moments later, Randy said, "Hey, here's a rest area. That's weird; it wasn't listed in the book. I'm stopping."

We bought a new book every year with current information, and it never failed us. Thinking nothing about it though, I pulled the spaghetti out of the fridge and flipped on the generator so I could use the microwave.

Randy stretched his legs, used the restroom, and jumped back in the driver seat. Fifteen minutes later, we ramped back onto the highway. Then we stopped. There was an accident within a hundred yards of the rest area. Randy prayed out loud.

Then he whispered, "Marli, close the blinds and don't let the kids look outside."

I knew it was bad. In fact, a body was in the median, covered with a sheet. We put a movie on for the kids and watched as emergency vehicles came from behind us. We sat for hours, watching the workers pry people from a pickup truck. The semi it had collided with was mangled as well.

It was one of the worst accidents we've ever seen. We talked to God, thanking Him for the rest area. I was grateful it wasn't us but felt awful for those involved.

The next morning, the phone rang. It was a man from Clarksville, Tennessee.

"Hello, Ernest," I heard Randy say.

His number was programmed in Randy's cell phone, and I knew it could be a long conversation. Ernest is a songwriter and calls us occasionally to sing over the phone. It was his goal to sing in all fifty states. Since he wasn't a traveler, he would call people in whatever state he needed and sing over the phone. We even called him from Ground Zero in New York City one time and let him sing a song he'd written just for that occasion. But that morning he didn't call to sing.

"Hey, I was praying for you and your ministry. Can I ask you a question?"

"Of course, go ahead," Randy said, wondering what was on his mind.

"Do you believe in visions?" Ernest asked.

"We do. The Bible says that young men will dream dreams and old men will see visions. So, yes, we believe," Randy told him.

"Well," he said, "last night I was praying for you, and the Lord showed me your RV humming down the highway. I saw hundreds of angels surrounding the RV. They were everywhere. So many, I couldn't even count them. I thought it was pretty cool."

"Ernest, you have no idea what happened last night."

Randy described the heart-wrenching accident and thanked him for praying for us.

I believe Satan wanted to kill us in that accident. I also know it seems as if we were favored over the people who died. Those are tough questions that can take a lifetime to resolve; some of them are never answered.

I can't explain why God doesn't stop every disaster from happening. But eventually, we have to mature enough to move past that question and trust Him with whatever. There may come a day that we are in an accident, and if so, He will still be God. One thing is for sure: I will always ask the Lord to send His angels to protect us.

When I read the Bible, I see a lot of godly people who went through horrific things. Satan uses disasters as weapons to destroy lives and tries to convince the world that God is cruel and unloving. Our enemy is out to rob, kill, and destroy. Sometimes he succeeds.

But his success is short-lived because a great day is coming.

No Weapon Formed Against Me

> But in that coming day no weapon turned against you will succeed. You will silence every voice raised up to accuse you. These benefits are enjoyed by the servants of the Lord; their vindication will come from Me. I, the Lord, have spoken! (Isaiah 54:17)

This verse confused me because history has proven weapons to be successful against believers; Christians have been persecuted and martyred for thousands of years. No matter how many times we quote this verse, somewhere in the world, followers of Christ are dying because they refuse to renounce Jesus. But the Lord told us not to fear what man can do to us. Matthew 10:28 says,

> Don't be afraid of those who want to kill your body; they cannot touch your soul. Fear only God, who can destroy both soul and body in hell.

In essence, Jesus tells us that there will be pain and some of us will be killed. Disaster may come, but we are not to fear, because it is temporary. We must focus on eternity instead of being so nearsighted that fear paralyzes us.

And paralysis is exactly what happened to me during my years of anxiety. I was dead in the water. I was terrified of disease, accidents, tragedies—anything that would hurt. During that time, I revisited Isaiah 54:17 and thought about it day and night.

But it wasn't until recently that I discovered something. God is definitely talking about a coming day when swords, guns, and any other weapons formed by man will be rendered useless, but as I quoted the passage yet again, the Lord questioned me.

He said, "Marli, what weapons does Satan use against you?"

Immediately I answered, "Fear, anxiety, worry, doubt, regret, shame, guilt, pride ..." My list went on and on.

God said, "That's right. But those weapons won't prosper because I won't let them. I will always rescue you—if you'll let Me."

I got excited with this new understanding of a verse I've known for years. It seeped into my soul, and my heart welcomed its truth as a dear friend. The Lord soothed me and showed me more:

> You can go to bed without fear; you will lie down and sleep soundly. You need not be afraid of sudden disaster or the destruction that comes upon the wicked, for the Lord is your security. He will keep your foot from being caught in a trap. (Proverbs 3:24–26)

God showed me that His main concern is guarding my soul. While life is precious and should be valued, eternity will last a whole lot longer than this life. If I believe that, crisis are no longer a threat to my contentment and peace and Satan's weapons of war are powerless over me.

I love God. He is my Savior and friend. He's also my therapist. Good thing He doesn't charge by the hour.

The Backseat View

Are you ready to ask yourself some questions? If so, swivel your chair and search your heart.

* Do you struggle with fear?
* If so, name the specific fears before God and ask Him to show you scripture to combat those weapons of the enemy.
* Has the enemy ever surrounded you?
* How did the Lord deliver you?
* Did the victory cause you to worship Him?

Whether or not you can relate to my particular experience, most of us struggle with something that's an obstacle to trusting God. It might not be fear or anxiety; it may be depression or an unhealthy ambition to succeed. It could be pride, or it could be rage. It might be addiction or unbelief. Ask the Holy Spirit to empty you of anything that tempts you to slide into the driver's seat and take the wheel.

WATCH FOR PEDESTRIANS

Airing My Dirty Laundry

Because people matter to God, they should matter to me. But sometimes I get distracted. In fact, I am regularly distracted. I'm not sure if it's because I get bored easily, or because I can be really selfish; maybe it's a little of both. I haven't figured that out yet, but while I lived in the RV, I learned a lot about people—and about myself *with* people.

God drove me to some places I wouldn't have gone if I had control of the steering wheel. I just wouldn't have gotten there—but I'm glad I did. Sometimes it wasn't enjoyable, but I ended up laughing at myself, which was good because I needed to relax. I thought I was already relaxed, but I wasn't. I was determined to make a difference in people's lives, but sometimes in the process I missed the *person.*

We were in a laundromat, washing about twenty loads of dirty laundry. I sent the kids back to the RV to catch up on homework. They were overwhelmed, I was overwhelmed, and Randy was grouchy because he was behind on scheduling concerts. We all needed to focus on something other than each other, and honestly, I wanted a couple of hours of solitude.

Then I realized that I had to do twenty loads of laundry *by myself,* and I got frustrated.

After enjoying my pity party for about fifteen minutes, I realized no one else was coming to my party. It was time to change my attitude, so I started praying. I didn't feel like it but did it anyway: *God, use me in the lives of people to bring them to You. So many don't believe, and they don't feel loved, and they're hurting. Take us where You want and help us follow.*

I was pulling loads in and out of machines and dropping quarters and spilling Tide, all while an old man kept telling me jokes I didn't understand. I acted like I couldn't hear over the tumbling dryers. His overalls were dirty, and I could tell he loved his greasy baseball cap.

I continued my silent prayer time: *Lord, please don't let me go through this season of my life without really seeing You in the everyday things. I so badly want to accomplish Your will for me and build Your kingdom. Use me, Lord.*

The old man leaned on the folding table I was using for my piles of clean clothes. He was muttering something, so I looked down to avoid a conversation. I was tired of shirts and jeans and underwear and solo socks. I was done—but not finished. In a single moment, God said to me, *Marli! If you don't pay attention, you will miss everything I have for you.*

He said my name so loudly that I couldn't miss it.

I looked up to see the old man in his veteran ball cap. In that moment, I knew what God wanted. I took a deep breath and exhaled. It felt good to slow down. Folding a sweatshirt, I tossed it on the table and gave the man my full attention.

"So did you serve in the army?"

He gave me details, and I thanked him. I was truly grateful for his sacrifice of serving our country. We talked until his clothes were dry, and then he walked away with a smile.

I relaxed. I changed my pace and started looking around. I chastised myself for my lack of compassion and focus. I saw people everywhere to encourage. And then, I laughed with God as I finished folding the last load.

Sometimes We Miss the Obvious

I'm not alone. I know it's not just me, because I live with three other people, and it happens to them too. I think most people get distracted somewhere along the way. Our minds wander from time to time, and we miss some really important things.

We've enjoyed visiting sites all across the nation. At the Saint Louis Arch, we bought four tickets to go to the top and see the view. Afterward, we watched a documentary film with actual footage of construction workers building the arch. It was intriguing.

About twenty minutes into the film, seven-year-old Kadison whispered, "Hey, Mom, is this a true story?"

"Son—are you kidding me? I just paid $12.50 for you to experience that true story."

But he'd missed it. Even though I got him there, took him up and showed him the view, he missed it. And I can understand; he gets it naturally. God has taken me to plenty of places multiple times because I failed to get it the first time around.

You probably know this, but the Israelites had an eleven-day journey to the Promised Land, which lasted forty years because they kept going around the same mountain. Generations were born, and an entire generation died. They got distracted along the way and veered off the road. If only they had let God lead, they would have gotten there a whole lot quicker.

But in the meantime, God used those forty years to teach them valuable lessons. He showed Himself as provider with supernatural food, clothing, and shoes that didn't wear out. I'll bet they were pretty sick of wearing the same outfit every day for four decades! I can't wait to switch out the clothes in my closet after a long, hard winter, but they didn't get to do that. They probably didn't get up in the morning and say, "Hmmm … what should I wear today?"

But I won't criticize them for getting sidetracked, because I've done the same thing over and over again. Somehow I get distracted, and all of a sudden my focus is blurred. I take a detour, and it adds time to my trip.

Maybe I'll get to heaven and the Lord will say, "Yeah, that RV trip only had to last six months, but you got distracted."

Sometimes We Get It Right

Kadison is the kind of kid with a lot going on inside. I can't always read him, which ironically enough has made us close. We talk. I ask questions. He answers—sometimes. Other times he just says "fine" and walks away. But he always says it in a Spanish accent. Not sure why, but both of my kids tend to deliberately speak with Spanish accents. It has become the norm around my house, though once in a while I'll ask that they please speak with the voice God gave them.

Anyway, Kadison has an innate sense of humor and is extremely particular, much like Randy. He came out that way. Even as a child, Kadison made us laugh. When he was five, I decided to get Christmas pictures taken. I dressed Kennedie in a velvet dress and Kadison in a pale gray suit with a matching tie. He looked adorable. (My mother always called him Joe Cool. She still does.)

Positioned in front of the mirror, his eyes got big.

"Mom! I can't wear this!"

"Why not, honey? You look very dapper," I said, knowing he had no idea what that meant.

"Because everyone is gonna think I'm the President."

"Of what?" I said, confused.

"The United States!"

I assured him the Secret Service was not needed, and President George W. Bush would not mind if someone confused the two of them.

He still makes me laugh, and I love when he shows his sensitive side.

A few years ago, I spoke at a women's luncheon to about seventy-five ladies. Randy and

Kadison came along, even though they were the only men. We did a few songs together before I spoke.

During my message, I noticed a woman with long red hair. She had a gigantic smile that lit up her whole face as she hung onto every word. When the program was over, I visited with a lot of women, and they told me how they'd enjoyed seeing a family lead worship together. The red-headed lady hugged me, with tears in her eyes, and whispered, "Thank you, and your son is very encouraging." I'd noticed Kadison talking to her for a long time while the three of us were packing up the sound system.

Finally, with all our goodbyes said, we pulled out of the church parking lot.

"Mom, did you see the woman with the red hair?" Kadison asked me.

"Yep. She was adorable—I don't think she was even a size two—and that smile! It covered her whole face."

"Did she tell you she has four kinds of cancer and only has one year to live?"

Everything went silent as we all stared straight ahead.

"No, honey. She didn't tell me that. In fact, I didn't talk with her very long at all."

I marveled that a teenage boy had ministered to a woman with terminal cancer. She'd chosen to tell *him* her story. I don't know whether she'd wanted to tell me or not, but in any case, Kadison had picked up the slack.

"Kadison, I am so glad you were there," I told him. "Great job noticing a woman who needed to talk."

New Life

We have no idea what people are going through or what burden they carry. It's impossible to tell at first glance, and if we aren't careful, we'll miss a great opportunity to show love. As a pastor once told me, "Whenever you meet someone, it's like walking into a meeting late. You have no idea what's been going on, and it is wise to observe." I don't always succeed in doing that, but I haven't forgotten the advice.

One time I walked into a service from the back of the auditorium. I saw a woman dressed in a grey sweatshirt with her hair pulled back in a tight ponytail. I welcomed her, even though I was the guest there. I like to meet people before a service starts; it relaxes all of us. Her face was long and tired, and I could tell she was miserable. I said to the Lord, *Set her free from whatever is holding her captive, Lord. Meet with her tonight.*

That was over six years ago, and she has become a dear friend. The Lord set her free from burdens she'd carried all her life. Maybe one day she'll tell her story. Until then, I'm honored to witness the incredible life-changing power of Christ in her.

Here's my point: That night, I *noticed.* I paid attention and didn't let the distractions of the moment pull me away from my mission. And a life was changed—but not because of me. New life was resurrected because of the transforming power of the Holy Spirit; I just got to watch. For a brief moment in time, I was a passenger in another person's car and witnessed life from her perspective. I saw God restore hope, offer healing, and administer deliverance.

Aisle Number Eleven

Other times, someone else's view is just plain depressing.

We had just finished a ministry-filled weekend. If I remember correctly, we'd had a marriage seminar on Friday night and Saturday, two Sunday morning concerts, and one evening concert. Three concerts on one day is a lot. Throw a seminar in there, and that's a recipe for exhaustion. I was sick of the sound of my own voice and felt like I'd been run over by a Mack truck.

It was late when we arrived back in our home area. Before getting to our destination, I suggested we stop at the grocery store and pick up some essentials for breakfast. The RV refrigerator was small and didn't allow for stocking up on much of anything. "Daily bread" took on a whole new meaning in the RV.

Randy dropped me off at the door of a twenty-four-hour grocery store. Kennedie and I grabbed two carts and split the list. No wandering aimlessly through the aisles of food, no wasting time. And I definitely didn't want to talk to anyone. I purposefully kept my head down to avoid eye contact. *Lord, I am totally spent. Done. Please have mercy on me and don't let me see anyone I know.* Sounds mean, but that's how I felt.

Kennedie went one way and I went the other while the guys waited in the RV. For some reason, I ended up in the spice aisle. I quickly lost my focus and got distracted looking at hundreds of spices. It felt good because it was another world that I knew nothing about.

I zeroed in on cream of tartar and asked myself out loud, "What would you use that for?" Other than cinnamon and garlic salt, I didn't use spices. Rarely did I cook. My kids said that I *assembled*. The line was "Thank you, Mom, for this beautifully assembled meal."

But as I stared at the cream of tartar, I heard a raspy voice from behind me: "Kid, kid—can you get me some black pepper?"

At least I knew about black pepper.

I saw an old lady, well into her eighties, standing behind me with a shopping cart full of food. I knew immediately that God was up to something. By this time, I was well aware that God refused to leave me as I was. He used every opportunity to teach me, fill me, challenge me—change me. *Please, God, let it be just a deep need for black pepper. Nothing more, okay? I am tired, and I want to go to bed. I have served all weekend, and I've got nothing left. Seriously, God, I mean it.*

I was rambling and complaining to the Lord in the middle of aisle number eleven. Simultaneously, I grabbed a few selections of black pepper ranging in quality, size, and price. I was helping the lady determine the best deal when suddenly she grabbed my arm, looked into my eyes, and said, "I'm lonely. So lonely. Do you know how lonely I am?" Even though her eyes filled with tears, my first thought was *Lord, surely there is another Christian in this huge store. I can't be the only one. Come on ... I can't even think of how John 3:16 goes.*

She grumbled about her miserable life, married to the same man for decades. "The only thing worse than being married to him is being alone," she confessed.

How sad. How tragic! All of those years should have added up to a wonderful life of companionship and a beautiful picture of Christ and the Church. But not here. Not in aisle number eleven.

As she poured her heart out and used the Lord's name in every way imaginable except that which honored Him, I gave the Lord my life again. I told Him, *Every day I give you me. I did it today too; you can have me. But, Father, I can't formulate a grammatically correct sentence right now. You've got to do this. I'll open my mouth, but you have to fill it. I don't know where to start, but I give you my time right now. Here we go; if you don't put words in my mouth, I'm gonna be standing here with a gaping hole in my face.* Then I started to speak.

Wanna know what I said? So would I. Truth be told, I have no idea. I have absolutely no recollection of words or even the content that tumbled out. But I remember being amazed at God's personal words for that woman.

I shouldn't have been, but I was shocked at how God ministered to her—an eighty-something-year-old woman, late at night, in the spice aisle. God was specific as He spoke through me, and I was rejuvenated, feeling the Holy Spirit physically use my body, and specifically my tongue, to reach her. It was exhilarating.

When I thought there was nothing more to say, I put my arm around her shoulder and said, "Let me pray for you." I purposely didn't ask permission; I just did it. I didn't want to give her the chance to say no. I asked the Lord to save her—save her soul, save her marriage, save her hope.

I hugged her and kissed her wrinkled cheek. I noticed she still took very good care of herself. Her skin was lightly powdered, and I could tell she was wearing perfume. Not *eau de toilette*, but real perfume—the kind you buy at the Macy's counter. She was a well-dressed lady whose long life only amounted to loneliness and disappointment.

As we parted, I noticed Kennedie at the end of the aisle. Unbeknownst to me, she had witnessed our prayer and embrace.

"You can't stop," she said. "You just can't stop!"

"Nope, God won't let me."

Leaking

I think we have evangelism all wrong—well, not *all* wrong, just *sorta* wrong. In our American churches, we set up programs, print flyers, perform stage plays. We have movie nights, potlucks, and special events. Those aren't bad, but if we depend on programs to lead people to Christ, we've missed the boat. That's one end of the spectrum.

The other end of the spectrum is becoming so much *like* the world (in order to reach it) that we end up becoming *part of* the world. In a moment, we get sucked into the culture and take on characteristics that we think are necessary to reach unbelievers. Jesus didn't do that. Even though He hung around with sinners, He didn't become like them. We do, and we are really messing this up.

Maybe we've tried to *do evangelism* instead of *live evangelistically*. Don't get me wrong; we've seen a lot of Christians evangelize effectively. But for the most part, we see a lot of believers who don't *believe* enough to evangelize. Many Christians think a relationship with Christ is too personal to talk about with others.

Beware—the enemy could tempt us into thinking, "Great, I don't have to talk about Jesus; I only have to show Him." St. Francis of Assisi is credited with saying, "Preach the gospel, and use words if necessary." I understand why so many use that quote; It's a great point, and I really like it. However, we shouldn't use it as a cop-out. Like most mottos, I think it has extreme value *in the right place*, but it should not be the mission statement of believers. We need words, as it's imperative that we give an answer for our hope (1 Peter 3:15). Souls are at stake, and we've got to step up to the plate and witness about Christ. Some of us have become so intent on "showing" Christ that we fail to speak about Him.

We need an authentic relationship with Christ that determines our lifestyle *and* our words. Simply put, we need both.

I have found that an intimate walk with Jesus fuels my witness. When I love Christ with all of my heart, soul, and mind, He flows out of me. I believe that to be passionately in love with the Almighty is the most effective form of evangelism. It's like filling a glass of water to overflowing; the water runs over the top and out of the cup.

What if we allowed God—invited God—to fill us to overflowing, and then evangelism became a fruit of that relationship? It is simple, but very powerful.

A cracked vase is useless. The water leaks out, and the flowers die. I would throw it out. But not God. He chooses and uses cracked vessels. He searches for those who want to be a container for His Spirit.

Because we're all broken in some sense, we all leak something. What do we leak? We leak whatever we're full of. If I am full of anger and resentment, I'll leak bitterness and rage. However, if I fill myself with the Truth, I will leak the fruit of His Spirit.

That's what happened to me in the spice aisle. He did it—not me. I couldn't do anything at that moment. I had no desire or energy to persuade anyone of anything. (I don't think that really works, anyway.) But I did make a choice to let Him use me. With compassion I listened to a hurting woman and then invited the Lord to use me to reach her. That sounds egotistical, but it's not. It's just the truth. That's the difference between taking credit for the work of God and simply laying down our agenda, laying down our lives—deciding to make good on our promise to be His disciples. When we do that, He uses us.

The Orchard

I am the true grapevine, and my Father is the gardener. He cuts off every branch of Mine that doesn't produce fruit, and He prunes the branches that do bear fruit so they will produce even more. You have already been pruned and purified by the message I have given you. Remain in Me, and I will remain in you. For a branch cannot produce fruit if it is severed from the vine, and you cannot be fruitful unless you remain in Me. Yes, I am the vine; you are the branches. Those who remain in Me, and I in them, will produce much fruit. For apart from Me you can do nothing. (John 15:1–5)

For me, this passage alleviates pressure. God doesn't expect me to do anything on my own. In fact, He says I can't. If I'm not attached to Him, I can't accomplish anything—of eternal value, that is. A lot of unbelievers are successful, but God's talking about accomplishing *His* will.

That's why it's so important that God drive my life. He decides what I need to do and where I should do it. I like how *The Message* translates this passage:

> Calling the crowd to join His disciples, He said, "Anyone who intends to come with Me has to let Me lead. You're not in the driver's seat; I am. Don't run from suffering; embrace it. Follow Me and I'll show you how. Self-help is no help at all. Self-sacrifice is the way, My way, to saving yourself, your true self. What good would it do to get everything you want and lose you, the real you? What could you ever trade your soul for?" (Mark 8:34–37)

I don't want to lose my soul just to get my way. I don't know about you, but I can be stubborn *and* ignorant at the same time. That's a really bad combination. It's frustrating to have a conversation with someone who doesn't know what they're talking about but is adamant anyway. We can be like that with God. He keeps trying to get us to slide over and let Him drive. Even when we do, we keep one hand on the wheel and yell for Him to go faster.

Clutch!

I learned to drive in an old Ford truck with a manual stick on the floor. Corb Albright, a longtime family friend who watched me grow up, taught me to drive. The truck would sputter and lunge forward as I fought to get the timing of the clutch and stick shift in sync. Patiently, he gave me directions as I stalled the engine again and again. It was hard, and I kept apologizing for grinding the gears. Honestly, I thought I was going to ruin the transmission.

"That's why we're in this old, beat-up truck. You're not ready for the good car," he told me.

I was taught to drive so I could go places by myself. (The first place I went was to get another car key made, just for me.) Driving gave me the independence to go where I wanted. I put my hands at ten and two on the wheel, stepped on the clutch, and put it into first. I learned to use the blinker, rearview mirror, and radio.

My first car was a little orange Chevette, and I loved being on my own; Corb and driver's training prepared me for that.

But that's not what life is like with God. He doesn't want us to take the wheel. He's not preparing us to drive off by ourselves so we can do whatever we want.

Someone once said, "Sin will take you places you never thought you'd go, keep you longer than you ever thought you'd stay, and cost you more than you ever thought you'd pay." Sometimes we make a mess of our lives and label it "God's will." Then we ask, *Why, God, am I miserable? Why is life against me?* I can hear God saying, *Hey, I wasn't driving. You were.*

That's why we should just go with Him.

I'll Meet You There

We were in California, heading to Minneapolis, Minnesota for a weekend of ministry. I was scheduled to speak at a youth retreat in Nashville, Tennessee, so Randy figured out how we could make it all work. He has always been a master at booking and is willing to drive through the night to get us where we need to be. But this time, I had to fly. So he dropped me off in Denver, and I caught a flight to Nashville. While I was at the retreat, he would drive to Minneapolis with the kids, and after I spoke, I would jump on a plane and fly out there to meet them. I remember how the goodbye conversation went:

"I would rather all go together," I said, as I held my carry-on suitcase.

"I know, babe, but we'll meet you at the Mall of America, and we'll have a couple days of rest before the weekend. It's gonna be fine," he said, and rushed me out of the RV before security flagged him. Airports don't like RVs in the passenger drop-off lanes.

I kissed the kids, jumped out, and watched as my house weaved through the airport traffic.

I made my way through security, grabbed a Starbucks drink, and sat down at the gate. I wondered why I'd said I would rather go together. Truth be told, I enjoyed being alone. I was completely comfortable navigating airports and changing planes and finding my host. It came with the territory and it was a refreshing break from the RV.

But as I got ready to speak a few hours later, I missed my family. I needed my family. I wanted to run ideas by Randy and pray together. I no longer wanted to be on my own.

The next morning, I flew to Minneapolis and took a shuttle to the Mall of America. Being our first time there, I wondered how we were going to find each other in such a big place. I mean, I know malls, but this is its' own little city.

I sat next to the window and took in the view. As the mall came into sight, I noticed the huge parking lots with thousands of cars. Then I saw the RV, parked along the edge of the lot. There was my home. Passing by it, I laughed and waved and then realized that people were looking at me. So, what? It surprised and excited me.

After stowing my suitcase in a locker, I met my family at the roller coaster.

"How did it go?" Randy asked. "Feel good about it?"

"Yeah, they really seemed to appreciate it. But I missed you. I like going together better."

And that's what God wants too. He wants to go *with* us. He meant for this trip to be taken together. Too many people decide to meet Him at the end and take the journey alone.

I think sometimes it's intentional but other times we grab the wheel without even knowing it. After a few miles, we feel comfortable in the driver seat, and the road is smooth, and the view is good, and we have a full tank of gas.

A lot of people go through life like that. They're so self-sufficient that they never realize their need for a Savior. I've always thought it is much more difficult to lead successful people to Christ than the down-and-outers. The poor are well aware of their need for help, but the wealthy can mask it with things. Fortunate is the man who has much *and* sits in the passenger seat.

Keep the Main Thing the Main Thing

As best as I tried to prepare for living in an RV, there was no way to know what we were in for. I could not imagine the highs, nor could I envision the lows. I tried to think of everything beforehand so I would be prepared, but it was impossible. I had never been there, and I didn't even know *how* to prepare. I did, however, call the IRS before we moved into the RV full time.

"Hi, my name is Marli Brown, and I just wanted to call and let you know of our plans. We are moving into our RV and will be traveling the country. Because of not having a permanent residence, all of our mail will go to my parents' house."

"Okay, how much money do you owe us?" the lady asked.

"Oh, we don't owe you any money; I just wanted you to know where you can reach us if you need us," I replied.

She laughed. "Honey, we are the IRS. If we need you—we'll find you."

This time we both laughed, and then she said, "But thanks for the call. You gave me a great story to tell at lunch!"

I wasn't trying to be funny; I was trying to be prepared. I was trying to think ahead to make the road smoother. But in spite of my efforts, there was no way I could prepare for everything God had planned.

That's why it was imperative that we let Him drive. He knew the way, and we were merely His passengers. God didn't give us directions and then abandon us; He went with us. He went *before* us, and hemmed us in from behind. He didn't leave us on our own, and He certainly didn't expect us to figure out where to go, how to get there, or what to do when we arrived. All we had to do was keep the main thing, the main thing. That's it.

What was the main thing? People. People are why we went. And that's why He came: to rescue people. He came as both a man and God—for us. He went through life just like we do, only He did it perfectly.

Jesus never looked at His Father and said, *Okay, I'll take the wheel. Let go, Dad; I got it.*

Read the Book

At the end of a Sunday morning concert, the pastor asked if we could pray for the sick. We asked if anyone wanted to be anointed with oil and prayed over. A lot of people came forward, but one woman in particular got my attention. She was crying and asked me to pray for her sister:

"My sister has nine brain aneurysms and is having surgery tomorrow at the University of Michigan Hospital. Can you pray for her?"

"Does she know Jesus?" I asked.

"I don't think so," she answered.

We anointed the woman with oil in place of her sister and asked God for a miracle. I asked the Lord to explode into the sister's life with His love, peace, and healing power.

That night, I couldn't get her out of my mind. I twisted and turned all night, asking the Lord to save her, heal her, and give her hope. Early the next morning, I picked up my Bible and did something I'd never done before and haven't done since. I said to the Lord, *I have been told that she doesn't know You. Could You give me a Bible verse to hang onto in her place?*

I didn't know what I was looking for or where to find it, so I flipped open my Bible and started reading. (I know really smart people say you shouldn't do that, but I don't believe them.) After just a few verses, my eyes fell on Psalm 3:3. David is referring to the Lord as "the One who lifts up my head."

I was excited. I thought, *Now if I were having brain surgery today, I would want God to lift up my head.* I had to tell her.

I borrowed a car and raced off to the hospital. Honestly, I didn't even know where I was going, but I kept following the blue *H* signs. Pulling into the parking lot, I asked the Lord to get me to the right area before they took the woman back to prep her for surgery.

I found the surgical registration area and stood in line to talk to the woman at the desk: "I am looking for a woman who is having surgery today." I said, giving only her first name.

"I'm gonna need a little more than that, honey," she said.

I felt unprepared; I didn't even know her last name.

"Hmm ... she has nine brain aneurysms. Does that help?"

"Sit right here, and when she comes through the line, I will point her out to you."

I sat down in a metal folding chair at the far end of the room and watched an endless line of patients register for surgical procedures. After about ten minutes, the woman at the desk pointed to a blonde lady walking to the opposite end of the room. I let the lady and her husband get situated and then walked over, clutching my Bible.

"Hi, my name is Marli, and you may tell me to leave. That's okay, but I have to tell you what I've been through during the past twenty-four hours for you."

They looked shocked and a little apprehensive as I explained about the lady's sister asking for prayer, about praying through the night, and finally about the verse I'd found. I opened my Bible and read it out loud.

Her eyes filled with tears, and she grabbed my hand. Just then, the nurse called her name. It was time to get prepped for surgery. I was out of time. I knew God could change that, but I didn't know how.

As they followed the nurse, her husband (a burly man who was actually a big teddy bear) turned and pointed at me.

"You—stay right there."

So I sat there and prayed. *God, I need more time. I want to tell her about your peace. Help.* Just then, the same nurse appeared and told me to follow her; "They want to see you."

When I walked behind the curtain, I saw her with an IV already in her arm.

I took her hand and said, "Are you scared?"

"Marli, you have no idea how scared I am. Do you realize the chances of me dying during this operation? I don't want to die."

"Well, I came to tell you about the One who can take all of your fear away," I answered her. "And if you give Him your life, He will reconcile you to God the Father, so if you do die, you will go to heaven." I hoped she understood the need to be reconciled to God.

She immediately said, "I want to go into this surgery knowing that God is okay with me and I am okay with Him. Does that make sense?"

"Absolutely." And then I explained how the blood of Jesus takes away all our sin. I also explained that His death on the cross paid the price for our sin. I told her that the Bible says we can be saved if we will call on His name. I asked if she wanted to give her life to God and give Him all of her sin.

"Yes. Will you help me?"

I don't remember the prayer, but I know she apologized to the Lord for her sin and asked for forgiveness. I know she told Him she believed and asked to be saved. I prayed after her and thanked Him for His salvation. I also asked Him to heal her body.

I knew our time was gone. They wheeled her to the operating room, and I gave her husband my phone number to call me after she was out of surgery.

She made it through the surgery, during which they removed eight of the nine aneurysms. Two weeks later, I visited her at her home. I took her a Bible and a devotional. I explained the importance of reading the Word and getting involved in a solid, Bible-believing church.

"I know you gave your life to the Lord on your deathbed. I believe you meant it, and I know the graciousness of God."

"Marli," she said, "it was so strange. The minute I asked Him to save me, I felt this warmth, this calmness, this … oh, I don't know what it was. But it felt great."

"Peace?" I suggested.

"Yes! That's it! Peace."

"That's because Jesus is the Prince of Peace, and He really loves you," I told her.

After a cup of coffee, I hugged her goodbye and left.

Two years later, she called me. I was in Dallas, Texas when my phone rang. After a few pleasantries, she got right to the point: "I have to be totally honest with you. Since you were here, I have not read my Bible, and I haven't gone to church. See, I am still disabled because of the remaining aneurysm, so I don't go out much. All I do is sit in my recliner and talk out loud to God. You never taught me how to pray, so I just talk to Him like I'm talking to you. I hope He doesn't mind."

"That's perfect! Don't let anybody tell you differently," I said, chuckling at her frankness. This woman's honesty was refreshing.

"Well, something strange is happening. After all this time, I think He is talking back to me."

"Probably," I said, this time laughing out loud, "He does that."

"But I don't understand what He's talking about. Can you help me?" she asked.

"I can try. What don't you understand?" I questioned, hoping I could at least point her in the right direction.

"One day, I was sitting in my chair, thinking. I said out loud to God, *Lord, I only ask one thing of You; when I die, I want to live with You in heaven forever.* Marli, as clearly as I hear your voice through the phone, I heard Him say, *Your name is in the book.* What book is He talking about?"

Instantly I thought of Revelation 21:27. "That's *The Lamb's Book of Life*! He's talking about *The Lamb's Book of Life*." I was astounded to hear how God spoke to her.

"God's got a book?" she asked, in utter surprise.

"Yes, God has lots of books, but He's referring to the one your name is written in."

I found it amusing that God had spoken to her about something she knew absolutely nothing about—and just waited for her to figure it out. I read the scripture to her so she could understand what He meant:

> So he took me in the Spirit to a great, high mountain, and he showed me the holy city, Jerusalem, descending out of heaven from God. It shone with the glory of God and sparkled like a precious stone — like jasper as clear as crystal. The city wall was broad and high, with twelve gates guarded by twelve angels. And the names of the twelve tribes of Israel were written on the gates. There were three gates on each side — east, north, south, and west. The wall of the city had twelve foundation stones, and on them were written the names of the twelve apostles of the Lamb. The angel who talked to me held in his hand a gold measuring stick to measure the city, its gates, and its wall. When he measured it, he found it was a square, as wide as it was long. In fact, its length and width and height were each 1,400 miles. Then he measured the walls and found them to be 216 feet thick (according to the human standard used by the angel).
> The wall was made of jasper, and the city was pure gold, as clear as glass. The wall of the city was built on foundation stones inlaid with twelve precious stones: the first was jasper, the second sapphire, the third agate, the fourth emerald, the fifth onyx, the sixth carnelian, the seventh chrysolite, the eighth beryl, the ninth topaz, the tenth chrysoprase, the eleventh jacinth, the twelfth amethyst. The twelve gates were made of pearls—each gate from a single pearl! And the main street was pure gold, as clear

as glass. I saw no temple in the city, for the Lord God Almighty and the Lamb are its temple. And the city has no need of sun or moon, for the glory of God illuminates the city, and the Lamb is its light. The nations will walk in its light, and the kings of the world will enter the city in all their glory. Its gates will never be closed at the end of day because there is no night there. And all the nations will bring their glory and honor into the city. Nothing evil will be allowed to enter, nor anyone who practices shameful idolatry and dishonesty—but only those whose names are written in the *Lamb's Book of Life*. (Revelation 21:10–27; emphasis mine)

For those who believe in Jesus, the Bible, and the power of His name, this is our future.

Home

I could have missed that opportunity to give hope to a hurting woman. I could have gotten distracted or let apathy make a different choice for me. But I didn't, and I got to witness an incredible miracle; a life changed by the power of God. A woman in need was my mission that day, and God drove me there. He gave me words of life to say.

He took me on an excursion that was life changing for both of us. She found the peace of God, and I found that once again He uses *people* to reach other people. It's His plan, and He invites all of us to go with Him.

It has been a joy and a life-changing experience for me to share my journey with you. With every year that passes, the memories fade but the miracles remain.

It is my hope that *my* testimony spurs you on to tell *yours*. Our adventures may look completely different, take alternate routes, and last for differing lengths of time. Your miles may be more enjoyable than mine, and my trip may include trials different from yours. But I know one thing that's the same: God wants to drive.

After eight years of living in the RV, we bought a house. At first, I was overwhelmed thinking about transitioning from the camper to a house, from life on the road to life at home. And once again, I was faced with the opportunity to let God do the driving while I sat in the front passenger seat.

We are still traveling and still serving in the same ministry. Our mission hasn't changed, but how we live has. Now I have my own washer and dryer, and they're my best friends. We have a place to return to and debrief. We have somewhere to study, practice, and prepare. We can spread out. The kids love their own rooms, and Randy and I have a lock on our bedroom door. We also have a new teddy bear puppy, Macy Lucille.

Life is good. Life is different, and God continues to stretch me. As I read through the pages I've written, I am still awed at what He has taught me. He was lovingly persuasive as He convinced me to travel with Him. I'm thankful for the journey, and yet a little disappointed I didn't learn more. As much as I tried to enjoy every season while I was in it, I'm not totally sure I did.

But tomorrow is a new day, and I'm sure I'll have another story to tell. Until then, I'll prop my feet up on the dash, ridin' shotgun, enjoying the view.

Randy & Marli Ministries

Randy and Marli Ministries is a non-profit 501c3 Worship Concert and Speaking Ministry. Based in Grand Rapids, Michigan, Randy and Marli Brown minister in churches nationwide and operate on a love-offering basis.

Randy and Marli have various recordings; including vocal, piano instrumental, as well as teaching.

Visit their website at: www.randyandmarli.com

- To place an order
- For information regarding a Worship Concert, Marriage Seminar or Ladies Event
- To schedule Marli for a speaking engagement, a Worship Concert, or a Marriage Seminar
- To support Randy and Marli Ministries with a one time or monthly gift.

Email: concerts@randyandmarli.com

Randy and Marli Ministries
PO Box 300221
Waterford, MI 48330

CPSIA information can be obtained at www.ICGtesting.com
Printed in the USA
BVOW08*0807070516

446951BV00001B/2/P